WOLFKEEPERS

A Wolfkeeper's Guide
to Training a Dog
by *Master Dog Trainer*
Toriano Antoine Sanzone

BookMasters, Inc.
Ashland, Ohio

WOLFKEEPERS

Master Dog Trainer Toriano Antoine Sanzone, B.A, provides a deep philosophical point of view on dog training and illustrates the complexities of raising a dog and the positive impact it can have on humans—spiritually, emotionally, and physically.
Book Design by Erik "Red E" Perez
Photos by: Tonia and Toriano Sanzone, Tamara Eston, Lynda Guillu, and Alberto Trevino
Editing/Typography by Susan Zyrkowski
Research: Angela Shparber and Brian Chau

BookMasters, Inc., Ashland, Ohio 44805
A BarakaJazz-Diesel Dog Book / August 2009

ISBN (hardcover): 978-0-692-00485-2

Library of Congress Cataloging-in-Publication Data
Sanzone, Toriano.
Wolfkeepers
Published simultaneously Worldwide
Printed in the UNITED STATES OF AMERICA

This book is dedicated to my grandmother,
Bettye Jean Williams Freeman, who proved to be
the ultimate Wolfkeeper as she lost her battle with lung cancer.
Your spirit lives deep inside my soul and
I dedicate this book to you.

The Dog as the Final Manifestation

I can meet a person's dog and within about 15 minutes of the first introduction, tell the person three things about his or her characteristics. The eyes of a dog reveal the pains and frustrations (or the happiness and contentment) of its owner. Our dogs act as a barometer—if most things are going right in our lives our dogs show it, and when things are not right in our lives, they show that, too. A dog is the purest embodiment of love, because it relies on pure primal instinct to base all its decisions. A happy and loving owner invokes a happy and loving dog. When you fix the dog you will fix the person, and vice versa.

–Toriano A. Sanzone (The Wolfkeeper)

This book belongs to Wolfkeeper:_____

_____

Dog's name:_____

Date: _____

This Wolfkeeper has successful completed Level I Training.

Signed by Master Wolfkeeper Toriano A. Sanzone:

_____

Contents

FOREWORD

When I was first told of Toriano's accident I immediately thought the worst. His ex-wife initially told me that the upper half and lower half of his body weren't connected and that his legs were devastatingly injured, and that Toriano probably would not live through the ten-plus hours of surgery he was in the midst of at the time. I was saddened beyond belief. Then, not two-and-a-half days later, I got a text message from a mutual friend telling me that Tori wanted me to call him. I was utterly confused; I knew he would need multiple surgeries over the next couple of weeks due to the nature of his injuries. I found out later that his injuries were not as catastrophic as initially stated, but a real risk to his life remained.

When I got ahold of Tori on his cell phone moments later I was elated that he was lucid. By no stretch of the imagination did I hear the positive, in-control Toriano I was accustomed to, but he was still "my" Tori and that made me hopeful. His psyche was hit harder than his body and he was grasping to make sense of the reality of his newfound surroundings.

I quietly listened to Tori as he wept through his initial thoughts during that first conversation; courageous thoughts that are validated in the following pages. Before hanging up I promised him that I would be there for him during this time of need. What that promise entailed neither of us knew at the time. No matter what, I was hell-bent on keeping that promise; it was up to Tori to stay alive long enough to allow me to.

Having been skeptical that Toriano would make it though the next stage of his recovery, after that conversation I felt that Tori at least had a fighting chance and, knowing him like I did, that's all he would need. That feeling was proven to be correct a few days later when Tori approached me about writing the introduction to this book. What the hell?! He was in a near-fatal collision not a week prior and he was already trying to write a book about it. That's the Tori I knew; relentless and determined to define his own destiny. I love him and wanted so desperately for him to recover. I immediately accepted, knowing that I wanted to be an active part of his recovery. However, I didn't know that his writing this book was going to be such an integral part of that recovery.

The focus that the writing of this book gave Toriano, for all intents and purposes, saved his life. I know that statement might seem like a stretch to some, but without that focus Tori would have been lucky to just barely heal his body; probably never once attempting to confront and conquer the inner demons that were keeping him from a full and rewarding life, both before and after the accident. Like a molting animal, during the process of writing this book Tori shed his unwanted layers and in doing so, for the first time in his life, is truly himself—a person and dear friend I am happy to finally meet.

I would like to let Tori know that I am honored to have played a small part in the writing of this book; a book which started out as a fairly straightforward account of his accident and subsequent hospitalization and blossomed into a deeply honest and incredibly candid story about a boy becoming a man and of that man taming his inner beast with the hopes of saving us all.

TIMOTHY LAWLER

PREFACE

I am a Master Wolfkeeper and Dogman, a dog lover, protector, and trainer, and mentor to those humans who want the same designation themselves. What is a Wolfkeeper or a Dogman (Dogwoman)? If you have a dog you can be a Wolfkeeper and a Dogman; this means you are a caretaker of one of God's greatest gifts to humans—the domesticated dog. We often trivialize how a dog can shape our lives and bring us joy.

Raising and training a dog is an art, like any other discipline. People get dogs without thinking about the full responsibility of ownership, and this is quickly manifested in the behavior of the dog. Every year 800,000 people are seriously injured by dogs, and ten to 20 people die every year as a result of dog bites in the U.S., with the majority of the victims being children. I consider this to be 800,000 untrained dog owners or people who should just not have a dog. My goal is to inspire the 48 million-plus dog owners in the United States to shed the label of "dog owners" and become "Wolfkeepers." Once you consider yourself a Wolfkeeper and start studying canine behavior and training your dog, you will find yourself transforming in the process as well, and becoming more in tune with nature.

I feel it is important for you to know that I wrote this original manuscript while lying in a bed for 68 days in Stroger Hospital. On June 22, 2008, I crashed my Lexus IS250 while trying to avoid hitting a motorcycle that cut me off in traffic. As a result of my car accident, I ruptured my right patellar tendon, broke my right femur in half, cracked my left acetabulum and greater trochanter, fractured my sternum, and, incredibly enough, suffered only minor head injuries. I had never experienced that level of pain in my life—I thought I was going to die. Lying in my hospital bed was a mental exercise every day, as I just watched the clock turn. I suffered multiple blood clots and had to teach myself how to walk again.

Almost as a form of therapy, I decided to write. What this has become is more than a dog training book; it is also a testimonial that anything is possible if your desire and passion are strong enough. Seven years ago, some senior dog trainers told me I wasn't good enough to train dogs. My entire life has been about defying the odds and powering through any obstacle. If it weren't for my accident, I would never have written this book. During that 68-day hospital stay, all I could think about was training my dogs and being around my dogs. I came to the realization that the reason God spared my life was to help train people to train their dogs. I also realized that the relationship between humans and dogs can go much deeper than the superficial "owner/dog" relationship. I thank God for my family and my dogs—without my love for them I might have given up and died right there in my hospital bed.

My best friend and advisor, Timothy Lawler, suggested I journal to keep from going crazy in the hospital. This manuscript started out as a journal, but turned out to be so much more. My accident gave me three months to think about my life, my family, love, the complexities of dog training, and their importance to me. I have met so many beautiful dog lovers over these last seven years and I hope this book makes them all want to become Wolfkeepers.

Tim, who wrote the foreword to this book, is from Minneapolis and was with me when Soldier, my Boxer puppy, was killed. Tim, like any true dog person, realizes that losing a dog is like losing a family member. Tim has been on the national heart transplant list for over two years, patiently waiting for a brand new heart while carrying 15 lbs. of equipment around on his hip. He was one of my many inspirations in writing this book, because one of the many traits of a Wolfkeeper is someone who has mastered the art of patience; he has truly proven to be a patient wolf while waiting for his heart.

Dogs can detect cancer and can reveal when people are near death; are used for search-and-rescue, guide dog, police, and military work; therapy, herding, guarding, hunting, and finally, most of all, to just be a companion. I know my dogs helped save my life, because I thought about them all the time while I was hospitalized. It would be great to have dogs in hospitals helping our ill, and we could if we utilized all the ancient and primal powers that dogs possess. Dogs have been integral to the lives of humans since the caveman, but we do not always treat these creatures with the respect that they deserve.

Almost every President in the United States has had a "first dog"; celebrities and socialites have for years paraded with their dogs on the red carpet; and over 48 million Americans are living with a domesticated "wolf" in their den. Most humans love their dogs, but we must now unlock the deeper essence of this love and transform it into the miracle it was always intended to be. Dogs can help change and save this world we live in, because they show unconditional love to their owners. Dogs don't care about anything except being loved and accepted by their pack; this simple concept needs to be adapted by human packs.

A Wolfkeeper is a human who, with kindness and purpose, has mastered the art of being Alpha in his pack. Our dogs yearn for the affection of their Alphas to guide them through the wilderness of our concrete jungles and navigate them to a place of serenity, while living in environments unnatural to the domesticated dog. It is my belief that as we train our dogs to change and to find their place in our crazy, mixed-up world that we will change ourselves in the process. I have trained a wide range of various breeds, from Yorkies and Affenpinschers to Korean Jindos, Black Russian Terriers, and Akitas, and have developed a multitude of training techniques and concepts to deal with any dog behavioral problem that may exist.

Wolfkeepers are those who have accepted a dog or dogs into their lives and have committed to offering their "wolf" the ultimate care, love, and training. There are dog owners and Wolf-keepers. A dog owner is a person who has a dog, but doesn't invest time, energy, or love into their dog. Dog owners just provide their dogs with shelter, food, and sometimes their attention, as long as it doesn't interfere with their favorite TV show. It's very easy to neglect our pets or take them for granted, just as it's easy to take our families for granted. However, when we break through and find love for and practice patience with our dogs we can also do the same with the humans in our world, and perhaps change our culture and how we treat each other as well.I can always tell when people don't really love their dog or don't care what's best for their dog. This is why I wrote this book—if we can find love for our dogs we can find love for those in the world around us.

TORIANO A. SANZONE

ACKNOWLEDGEMENTS

Thank you, God, for allowing me to be a keeper of your precious flock, the domesticated dog; and thank you for giving me the passion to help people and change their lives through their dogs.

Thank you, Bettye Jean Williams Freeman, for being my best friend and raising me to be the best man possible. If it weren't for your unconditional love for your family none of this would have ever been possible.

I would like to acknowledge all the members of my family, who have made me the ultimate Wolfkeeper. I would like to especially thank my great-grandparents Murray and Clarice Reed, who bought their first dog for $5 back in the 1940s (an Airedale named Joe). I would like to thank William, Gladys, and Stephanie Buford for always having a deep love for all the dogs that they have owned over the years and sharing that with me. I thank my mother, Tonia Sanzone, for exposing me to so many dogs early in my life and for sharing her passion for dogs with me. I thank my Aunt Tammy for making my dreams financially possible and for believing in me when the outside world refused to. I would like to thank my Aunt Towuana as I continue to follow her swagger, I thank my cousin Tino for being Tino, and thank you to my sister Shantae and my little cousin Diana for being my interns.

Most importantly, thank you to my sons, Jazz Klyne and Baraka Paris Sanzone (future Presidents and Wolfkeepers in training), for inspiring me to be the best dad on the planet—I know you two will be the greatest Wolfkeepers ever one day. Thank you, Melyssa and Indiigo. Thank you to Zac&Zan, Big Tim Dog, ANR, OB, Crazy Shawn, David Jones, Troy Lewis, Shannon Gillespie, GAC, K-Town for molding me, and everyone I know and love, too many to mention (2500# in my BlackBerry). Extra thanks to Susan Zyrkowski and Erik Perez for making this book a reality. Rest in eternal peace Bettye Jean Williams Freeman, Carol Davern, and Natalia Vynnochuk, whom I lost while writing this book.

I would like to thank all the families and individuals who have allowed me to come into their lives and homes and share my passion for and knowledge of dogs with them. I would also like to thank all the dogs and puppies that I have met over the years—thank you for each life lesson and training lesson you left with me so I could teach the next wolf. Peace and Love to all my fellow Wolfkeepers and to all the Master Dog Trainers who shared their knowledge and skills with me and helped make me a better Wolfkeeper. I would like to thank my mentors, who filled in the blanks for me and helped me hone my dog training skills: Master Michael Straton, Lori Berg, Master Walter Ward, Master Oliver Grey, and Master James Morgan. I would like to thank all of the thousands of pet professionals whom I have met and who have helped me gain a deeper knowledge of training and the dog industry as a whole. I would like to thank the Global Dog Nation for reading this book and joining us on our mission to change the world by changing people through their dogs. I love you all.

I would also like to thank all the people who have been in my life over the past 34 years and have shown me love during my most difficult and trying times. Most importantly, thank You, God, for giving me my mother, Tonia Sanzone, who loved to train dogs ever since she was a child, because I can truly say that I was born into the game.

Finally, I must acknowledge my number one dog, Joe Diesel—the greatest dog ever, who taught me more about life than I ever thought possible from a doggie.

Your Fellow Wolf,

Toriano A. Sanzone
Circa 2009

"Born into the Game"

Toriano Sanzone, a young Wolfkeeper

CHAPTER 1
THE WOLFKEEPER
THE BEGINNING

My mother and great-grandmother would bathe their dogs in the bathtub with us as children, so as a toddler I actually accepted our dogs as my siblings!

I was first introduced to dogs by my mother, Tonia Sanzone, when I was four years old. She began training and breeding Afghan Hounds with her friend Julia in 1978 in Bellwood, Illinois. As I grew up I observed dog behavior firsthand and by default, because there were always at least four dogs in my household. I quickly acquired a fondness for dog hair and dog poop! By 1978, there were two Afghan Hounds, a Poodle, and a Doberman in our small three-bedroom house. My mother would find strays on the street and take them in.

My family has always loved dogs, and I feel that God intended for me to be a shepherd of this amazing creature. My grandmother Bettye Jean told me that my great-grandfather bought an Airedale Terrier for $5 when she was a child, which she said back in those days was a lot of money. At that time people didn't register dogs and weren't so concerned about their dogs being purebred—they just wanted a family pet or a guard dog. Growing up in Chicago in the 70s, I only remember our dogs living outside. We would let our dogs inside if the weather was extremely bad, but for the most part our dogs were allowed to bear the elements of the urban environment and the Chicago climate.

My grandfather raised Beagles that lived in a shed year-round and were strictly for breeding, unlike the modern Beagle that lives in a condo or a comfortable house. I lived in Kenya in East Africa for a time, and there were dogs there that were completely contained in boxes all day, unable to see out, and were only let out at night to patrol the grounds for intruders.

My family has always had a deep, affectionate love for their dogs. My Aunt Tammy thinks that her 120-pound Presa Canario, Chance, is a human. She built a doggie condo for him out of three crates, complete with a satin pillow, water bowl, and private television. Chance also has a diaper bag for when he travels and his very own doggie seat belt for when he rides in Tammy's Camaro.

My mother and great-grandmother would bathe their dogs in the bathtub with us as children, so as a toddler I actually accepted our dogs as my siblings! I was an only child and my closest friends in 1978 were our four dogs. I recall reading and studying every dog training book and animal psychology book I could get my hands on at an early age.

As a teenager growing up on the west side of Chicago, I studied the history of all the local dog trainers and was fortunate enough to work with some of the greatest Master Dog Trainers to ever live in Chicago: Tonia Sanzone, Demetrice Weathersby, James Morgan, Walter Ward, Michael "Gypsy" Straton, Oliver Grey, and a host of others.

One of the proudest moments of my life was in 1996, when I purchased my first dog by myself—my first professional demonstration dog, a Boxer puppy I named Soldier. I was living in Minneapolis, Minnesota at the time—this is where I started my professional journey of mastering dog obedience and canine behavioral modification. This was a special time in my life, because I had graduated from Gustavus Adolphus College in Saint Peter, Minnesota, and had just left my corporate job after one year due to my dissatisfaction with working for someone else. I had all the time in the world to train Soldier. My mother said, "I sent you to college to learn to pick up dog poop?"

When I got Soldier, any book I hadn't already read about dog training I found and read. I loved that dog so much, and all summer literally all I did was train Soldier. I loved talking to my breeder; I loved shopping for Soldier; and I loved the pure enjoyment of having my very own dog. I had no family when I lived in Minneapolis, so Soldier was my only family member. Just like when I was a child, I had a brother again—my dog.

Soldier was significant in my training career because of a fatal error that I made, which led to his death when I left him unattended in my backyard. Soldier, along with my upstairs neighbor's six-month-old Boxer puppy, were hit by a car when they got out of the yard. I will always blame myself for that accident and to this day, I never leave my dogs unattended. A big part of dog training is teaching our companions how to survive in the urban environments we have placed them in. First lesson of dog training—never leave your dog unattended! I treat my dogs like my children and keep a close eye on them at all times.

In 2002, I acquired my second professional demonstration dog—a Johnson-Scott all-white American Bulldog named Joe Diesel, which I got from a breeder named Chris Ellis in Fowlerville, Michigan. With this dog, I began my journey in helping families and individuals professionally train their dogs to the highest level of perfection. I chose an American Bulldog as my demonstration dog because I wanted a challenge in pushing to the maximum a dog not known for its intelligence.

They say you only get one great dog to come into your life. Well, if that's true, Joe Diesel is it. He is one of the most amazing living creatures that I have ever encountered, and his intelligence and skill-set surpass that of any dog I have engaged in training. Living with Diesel for seven years has bolstered my belief that dogs are so much more capable than what we give them credit for.

I am a Wolfkeeper, which means training dogs is my life and my passion. I have dedicated the last seven years of my life to studying dog behavior and teaching people to be better caretakers of their canine companions; but I feel as if I have been doing this as long as I have been on the earth. The world is waiting for more Wolfkeepers to shed their old skin and come alive and help change the universe by mastering the art of training a dog. However, training a dog takes a lot of patience and constant practice. Much like raising a child, Wolfkeepers must consistently work with their puppy/child a little bit every day.

As I lay trapped in my hospital bed, unable to walk for 68 days after my auto accident, I felt like a dog being kenneled for the first time, about to undergo weeks of doggie boot camp. I felt like a wild wolf being contained in a zoo, learning patience by default, trapped inside of its cage. So, like the dog and the wolf, I had to learn patience. I experienced what my friends at Westville State Prison to whom I teach dog training, must experience every day; locked away in their cells, they are also learning the art of patience.

The only thing that got me through that long hospital stay was my burning need and passion to get back to my wolf pack. I never realized how much I loved my family and my dogs until I was away from them for 68 days. (One of my best friends, Lee, proved to be a great friend indeed when she snuck Stella the Affenpinscher into my hospital room!) Yes, for me owning a dog is that deep; deeper than I will ever truly understand, and it can be that way for you too.

The relationship between man and wolf goes back to the beginning of our time here on earth. Dogs have worked hard for us since their domestication and continue to do so; they lead us and function as guardians—our eyes and ears to protect us and our belongings; they act as our friends and give us unconditional love and affection; and they don't ask for very much from us in return.

After reading this book, if you put its principles into practice, you will transform yourself from simply being just a dog owner to becoming a great dog trainer, or Wolfkeeper—a person deemed by the heavens to partner with the dog that God has placed in your life.

CHAPTER 2
DOG
ADDICTION

At one point in time I had up to ten dogs in my home in doggie boot camp. I was only supposed to have one dog in my two-bedroom apartment, so I had to smuggle the other nine past my landlord every day.

I remember wanting to become a dog trainer when I saw the movie *The Amazing Dobermans* back in 1978. I was absolutely fascinated by how well-trained these dogs were—the obedience they demonstrated and the tricks of which they were capable. After seeing the movie, all I wanted to do was set up agility equipment in my backyard and teach my dogs how to jump and crawl on command. I saw Mel Gibson's movie *Mad Max 2* and fell in love with his sidekick Australian Cattle Dog, named simply "Dog," and fantasized about traveling the U.S. in a Corvette Stingray with my faithful road dog. Later, I enjoyed the movie *I Am Legend* with Will Smith, because I saw myself walking the empty streets of Chicago with my American Bulldog, Diesel, fighting vampires.

I grew up loving every component of owning a dog. I didn't mind the smell of dog poop and I loved getting our kennel area ready for any new dog that we adopted into our family. I loved going to the pet store with my mom and paying $25 per week until we paid for the Shih Tzu puppy that we had on layaway. I was always so excited to go buy dog toys and pick out dog food, but had no idea that one day this would be my full-time career and life's passion.

The first time I saw a professionally trained dog was in 1983, when my family went to a kennel in the country to purchase a fully trained German Shepherd named Rebel. I recall being amazed by the level of control the dog trainer asserted over his attack dog, and his ability to turn the dog on and off like a light switch.

The first dog I tried to officially "train" was a Boxer named Brandy, which my mom bought for me in 1986. I would read my little dog-training book and then go attempt to train Brandy using the techniques in the book. I loved Brandy so much, more so because it was the first time I felt like this dog was all mine. I would walk her every day after school and let her sleep in my room. It was one of the saddest days of my life when Brandy was taken from me by my stepfather, who seized her in the divorce between my mom and him. I realized then, at the tender young age of 13, that losing a dog is like losing a human, whether to death or desertion, and even after all this time I have never gotten used to it.

In 1996, I acquired the first dog I ever purchased for myself—a Boxer named Soldier, and this was the first dog that I trained completely by myself. Soldier was such a special dog to me and I loved him with all my heart. My girlfriend at the time, Autumn, used to travel one hour every week out to the country to visit our puppy before I could afford to take him home. One day I came home and as I walked in Autumn yelled "Surprise!", and there was Soldier, sitting on the couch—she had picked him up for me. I loved that dog almost like a child, and he had a major impact on me wanting to become a dog trainer. I used to walk around Minneapolis with him and train him on the street so much that people would ask me if I was a trainer. I realize now that I have always just had a love for the game and had no idea that it would ever become a career. I just did what I loved, and everything else was a by-product of my passion for and obsession with dogs.

After Soldier was hit by a car and killed, I vowed to teach all my future dogs extreme obedience, and I would later add a vow to teach humans how to better train their dogs. Around that time I met another professional dog trainer, and that's when it all fell into place for me. I knew that I wanted to be a professional dog trainer, or what I refer to now as a Wolfkeeper.

I had always joked that when all was said and done, I was going to move to the country and start a dog farm. Well, after ten years in Minneapolis in the music industry doing marketing and promotion, I was fired from my job for freelancing for another record company—one week after my son Baraka was born to my then-wife, Melyssa, and me. I moved back to Chicago with my family, into my grandmother's two-flat where I grew up.

For about two months, I searched for jobs, not knowing exactly what I wanted to do. Then, one day, just like that, I decided that I would work with dogs. I had seen an advertisement in the job section in the newspaper looking for a kennel attendant and went down for an interview. I got the job and was in charge of riding in a van throughout Chicago and picking up and dropping off dogs for doggie daycare.

During my doggie daycare days, I learned a lot as I extracted sometimes-unwilling wolves from their dens. I observed dog behavior daily as I acted as the shepherd for over 70-plus dogs running around a 10,000-square-foot warehouse. I broke up numerous dog fights and had to care for many injured dogs due to this failed concept of doggie daycare. It is not natural to force a group of dogs to play together in what we consider a social environment. Doggie daycares and doggie parks create multitudes of behavioral problems and should only be used as environments to test/prove obedience training.

While I was working at the doggie daycare, I also started working at a dog training facility, and studied my mentors closely for two solid years. In addition, I volunteered at Animal Care and Control and various other shelters in order to hone my dog training and observation skills. I trained a wide variety of dogs and talked to lots of different families and individuals until I felt extremely confident in my dog training skills. I started off by going to people's homes and having small group classes, and then I started running doggie boot camps out of my home. At one point in time I had up to ten dogs in my home in doggie boot camp. I was only supposed to have one dog in my two-bedroom apartment, so I had to smuggle the other nine past my landlord every day. This forced me to quickly train eight to ten dogs at any given time not to bark, not to pee/poop in the house, and how to get along in my wolf pack. When you live with ten dogs that all have behavioral problems, you are forced to be the Alpha leader!

Most households lose control over their family pet because no one in the household has assumed the role of Alpha leader. When the pack hierarchy is controlled by the dog, that household is living with a dangerous dog that will eventually challenge or bite another family member or stranger out of dominance. While it's happening, most people don't realize that their dog has taken the role of Alpha leader of the house, and they will eventually get rid of the dog in order to take back control over their pack. Excessive barking at strangers, having to put the dog away when guests come to visit, any form of aggression towards humans or other animals, and separation anxiety are a few examples of how your dog has gained Alpha status in your pack. In some instances the behavior is so extreme that the assistance of a professional dog trainer will become necessary.

CHAPTER 3
REFLECTION OF THE 80S DOG

I hope to one day educate people who exploit dogs to realize the destruction they cause when they abuse God's creatures.

I worked in marketing and promotion for ten years with brilliant music artists, but nothing I've ever done for a living could compare to my love for training dogs. Why dogs? Because, while growing up in the North Lawndale neighborhood in Chicago (also known as "K-Town"), my family always had dogs. At that time, our dogs only lived outside. Today, you will seldom see or hear about a dog living outside in a major city, as the laws for the rights of dogs have gotten better over the years and continue to progress.

I think about our German Shepherds my great-grand-mother Queen Clarice just loved to death, and how she would brush her dogs' teeth and gargle their throats with Listerine. Our dogs were very loving just like my great-grandmother, but could also be mean as hell just like her if pushed or challenged by out-siders. Our dogs had a history of multiple attacks on intruders, but they completely displayed the mentality of my family growing up on the west side of Chicago. What's inside the human will be inside the dog, because we project our fears and/or our peace onto our dogs. This is why the relationship between man and dog is beau-tiful when both become balanced.

Back in the 80s in Chicago, dogs lived outside and ate table scraps. This was many years before the age of the fancy condo dog. Now, dog food and vet care for an animal can cost hundreds of dollars per month, and we have dog parks, dog-friendly bars, dog daycare, dog beaches, and dog-friendly cafés. People are starting to really love their dogs, and our world is becoming more dog-friendly.

I can say that I have seen every level of treatment of dogs. I have always hated witnessing abuse to dogs, and saw a lot of abusive things happen to dogs while I was growing up. I remember an elderly black man named Moe, the unofficial dog trainer of my neighborhood, who used to tie Pit Bulls to fences and agitate them with belts in order to get them to become protection dogs. This is something that you won't often see in any neighborhood in America today, at least not out in the open; however, back in the 70s and 80s people's mentality toward dogs was completely different. I remember seeing my next-door neighbor Pete fight his Doberman, Prince, against other dogs and the day Prince almost killed Pookie's German Shepherd, Pup Pup. Yes, back in the 80s in Chicago people would fight dogs on street corners for sport. I recognize now that this was part of the culture and was a way of life for certain people. As I think back, I wonder how people's mentality sank to this level of inhumanity toward dogs.

I recollect a guy named Jerome putting Pit Bull puppies under milk crates and poking them with sticks in order to make them tough and aggressive. There was a black and gray German Shepherd that lived next door tied up to a raggedy black dog house his entire life. Old Man Homer would only let him loose at 11 p.m. and only for a short time. The mother of my friend Renee had a boyfriend who used to light marijuana inside of pop bottles and lock their Pit Bull in a closet and force him to get high before he would fight him against other Pit Bulls. I recall my mother rescuing a black Afghan Hound from some cruel kids who had put a wire around his neck and were throwing rocks at him. Once, someone poisoned all five of our German Shepherds, and I remember wondering how some people could be so heartless to dogs.

There has always been a strong fondness for dogs, even by people who have used them for illegal purposes. I hope to one day educate people who exploit dogs to realize the destruction they cause when they abuse God's creatures—not only to the dogs, but to themselves as well. However, as long as it still occurs, we as a society and as Wolfkeepers must fight to stop the abuse of dogs.

Regardless of all the abusive things that I saw happen to dogs while I was growing up, it didn't corrupt my feelings for them.

I maintained a deep love and passion for dogs. I've also come to realize that animal abuse comes in many forms. In our modern world, I consider it abuse for a dog to be locked in a cage in a condo for eight to ten hours a day, or to allow a dog to become obese, or for a toy breed to never go outside. Dog abuse comes in many shapes and forms, and I believe there is not much difference between a guy like Jerome poking puppies with a stick and condo-owners leaving their dogs caged for 10 hours a day—it is still mistreatment of their dogs.

A Wolfkeeper is a person who will work to ensure that their dog and dogs around them are properly taken care of and loved. When a person develops love for a dog, they will find it easier to develop love for their fellow human. We could change the world if everyone loved a dog and worked to master the art of owning a dog properly. I wish I could travel back in time and teach all those people who used to abuse dogs how to love and care for them instead.

I have always had a desire to train dogs and to get them to do tricks on command. Little did I know that many years later, I would dedicate my entire life to changing people through their dogs and pursue a career in protecting dogs from abusive people and changing people who abuse dogs into Wolfkeepers. It wasn't until Monday, June 23, 2008, one day after my car accident, that I realized that I had become a Wolfkeeper. As I lay in my hospital bed day after day, I thought about dog training and how it had kept me physically and mentally fit. Quite often a doctor would ask me if I worked out or was an athlete. "No," I would reply; "I train dogs." I never thought I would become what I am today—a lone wolf in search of 48,000,000 wolves to join me on this journey.

CHAPTER 4
WHAT TRULY IS
A WOLFKEEPER?

A Wolfkeeper is a person who is Alpha in every aspect of their world and exhibits control over their dog, whether it's a Yorkshire Terrier or a Japanese Akita.

We should abandon the concept and term "dog owners" and start calling ourselves "Wolfkeepers," so that we can embrace the seriousness of the responsibility of owning a dog. Dogs administer serious bites every year because they are owned by weak dog owners. A Wolfkeeper is a person who is Alpha in every aspect of their world and exhibits control over their dog, whether it's a Yorkshire Terrier or a Japanese Akita. Raising a dog is like raising a child; they both need rules and structure. When you don't provide your dog with either, you will eventually have an animal that you cannot control and it will either destroy or be destroyed. If the Alpha leader is weak there will be complete chaos within everyone in the pack.

The family pet seeks an Alpha wolf because we have made them dependent upon us by domesticating them. Our dogs don't wake up before sunrise and go hunting for food—they wait for us to put pieces of kibble into their bowl. The modern dog is not allowed to figure out pack order by running in the wild with a group of dogs and pups—we have contained them as single dogs living in our homes. These single dogs living in our homes or condos yearn for a leader, but we have deprived them of true pack culture for thousands of years. Our lack of understanding of true pack culture is part of the reason why we have so many dog attacks every year.

When I go into the prison system and work with the inmates to teach them how to train dogs, I can sense their thirst for structure and discipline; not just the inmates, but the dogs as well. The dog is to man as sword to samurai warrior. When a handler and dog are completely in sync, you cannot separate the dance from the dancer.

Dogs want a leader, but sometimes a leader can be too tough and the dog might bite somebody in the family out of fear; they respect/fear the owner, but not their child[ren]—I call this "Dad's Dog." There are dogs that have extreme separation anxiety because the owner cuddles the dog too much or showers all their attention on the dog because they have lost a loved one or are lonely in their human pack relationships. Some dogs become extremely aggressive because the owner honestly has no clue how to control the dog and didn't do research before acquiring that particular breed. For example, a person may decide to own three male Pit Bulls while living in a two-bedroom apartment, erroneously thinking that there is absolutely nothing wrong with confining three male gladiator dogs to a small space.

There are dog owners who secretly find power in owning and living with an out-of-control or aggressive dog because it makes them feel powerful; plus the dog looks good in their Range Rover. There are dogs that don't have complete separation anxiety but are allowed to get away with murder because they aren't provided with rules and structure; i.e., the dog that usually sleeps in the bed and gets kicked out when the boyfriend starts sleeping over, but then has to be allowed back into the bed because it will bark all night otherwise. There are also dogs that become weak and sickly because they're not allowed to just be a dog—have never been outside in the rain or played in the snow unless they have on booties and a coat, have never been boarded, and live such a plush life that they have lost all of their wolf essence and haven't developed any resistances. This is why sometimes the good old alley dog lived forever, while now fancy condo dogs spend most of their lives on medication.

Another characteristic of a Wolfkeeper is a person who strives to find the proper balance in raising a particular breed in a particular urban environment. For example, a Yorkie living in a house in Beverly Hills will require different rules from a Yorkie living in a condo in Chicago. The Beverly Hills Yorkie will have great weather working for it so it can be completely trained to go outside—versus the Chicago Yorkie living in a condo, and which might need to be trained to go in a litter box or on pads due to the weather. The Beverly Hills Yorkie must exhibit café etiquette, because due to the nice weather it will frequently be able to travel with its leader. The Chicago Yorkie will require learning elevator etiquette and must learn how to walk on busy Chicago streets. Wolfkeepers must completely understand what training skills are necessary to their particular dog in their particular environment.

When it comes down to it, the biggest question is "Who's the boss?" Who will take charge over the pack and lead the pack through the urban wilderness to safety? Does the pack respect the appointed leader enough to follow the pack rules, or is there always insubordination from the other wolves? There can only be one Alpha in every pack, so if you have a dog the short answer is, "You should be the boss, not your dog." Our dogs' safety and happiness are dependent upon this clear delineation—if not, disaster may lurk around the corner and the cost might be too high to ever recover from even one mishap. If you have a dog you are your dog's Wolfkeeper, and you must be the fearless, undisputed Alpha leader of your pack.

CHAPTER 5
DOG NATION

When we come together as 48 million dog owners we will be able to help people all around the world; financially, politically, and spiritually.

We are here to train all 68 million dogs and the 48 million people who are their keepers. Can you imagine if all 48 million dog owners in the United States banded together and formed a Wolf Nation? Can you imagine the political influence we could assert within our government? I truly believe that during this Obama era, we can create our own era and mold our own destinies. What is an "era"—when one idea dominates a period of time? Well then, let us create the "Era of the Wolfkeepers," and during this era dog owners across the country will master the art of dog training and in the process become more spiritual people—physically and mentally connected to the world around us. Ghandi said that our culture will be judged on the treatment of our animals. It follows, then, that if we can teach 48 million people to become sensitive to the needs of their puppies and dogs, then those 48 million people will be more sensitive to the needs of their neighbors.

Imagine a world where dogs are sitting off-leash at cafés and walking through malls with their masters. I can visualize a world where dogs are a necessity in our day-to-day tasks. We will use them to walk with our children home from school, to locate cancer cells, to guide a family out of a burning building. Many dogs died or were injured in the aftermath of the September 11th, 2001 World Trade Center attacks, searching for victims for days, as their paws became bloody from walking on debris and their lungs were filled with suffocating dust clouds. I sincerely believe that if we as Wolfkeepers form a grassroots organization consisting of 48 million united dog owners, we will be able to inspire the President himself to listen to our political agendas as a coalition of peaceful warriors.

We live in dangerous times, and there will never be a better time to begin to enlist our canine companions to once again guide us to safety through these urban jungles. A dog is man's best friend—trite but true; but even better, a dog is part of a person's life source and the final manifestation of what's happening in that person's life. If you are happy you will have a happy dog. If you are angry you will have an angry dog. God gave us dogs in order to gauge where we are as individuals and to help us enhance our own well-being.

When we come together as 48 million dog owners we will be able to help people all around the world; financially, politically, and spiritually. Don't be blasé about your dog, because it's more than just an item you pass by while walking to the kitchen. Dogs are emotional creatures that have the ability to surpass all your expectations. A dog can and will enhance your life and the lives of those in your pack.

Our country is currently recovering from economic disaster and was apparently on the brink of complete financial pandemonium. However, the pet industry is a $68-billion industry, and it can help rejuvenate our nation's economy. We spend millions of dollars every year in economic damages caused by dogs, because every year 800,000 people are seriously injured from dog attacks. Picture this—if we trained these 800,000 dogs next year *before* they bit, that would be 800,000 people who would not have to spend money on medical bills, nor be traumatized by their experience. What about the dog bite victims brought to county hospitals who can't pay for their medical bills? You, the taxpayer, pay for that dog bite, so you would save money also.

If we train 800,000 additional dogs per year that aren't currently being trained, it would require an army of Wolfkeepers to train them, which would in return create multitudes of new jobs. In addition, if you educated 800,000 neglectful dog owners and transformed them into Wolfkeepers, you would have people who in the past wouldn't spend much money on their dogs, but now will. Therefore, you would see an increase in vet care, grooming, pet supplies, doggie daycare services, dog walking services, dog training services, and dog boarding. We would also save revenue that currently goes to our animal care and control services because fewer dogs would become strays and fewer dogs would be euthanized due to being vicious or simply lost. We would spend less money on plastic surgery, because out of the 800,000 dog bites each year 44,000 are face bites to children, which averages 121 bites per day. Homeowners would save money by paying lower homeowner insurance premiums for certified trained dogs. Dog owners across the country would save money by having well-trained dogs, because the dogs would no longer habitually destroy personal items like cell phones, shoes, and expensive furniture. All of this money saved could go to help people in dire need of food and shelter. We should not live in a country where people are hungry and homeless, and our Wolfkeeper Nation could fix many of the problems of the world around us—this I know to be true.

I want to teach people how to become dog trainers and make them realize they don't have to be just dog owners, but can be Wolfkeepers. People need to realize that the connection between human and dog is very spiritual and deep, which is what God intended. My belief is that the Wolfkeepers can and will change the world through their highly trained dogs.

We can all agree that the world around us needs to change for the better as soon as possible. We can make one simple change by teaching prison inmates how to train dogs. I work with a program called "Mixed-up Mutts" at Westville State Prison in Westville, Indiana, and I have seen firsthand the tremendous power of the dog over human conditions. There are not too many situations as intense as being incarcerated and having your body, mind, and soul institutionalized for a number of years. However, I have witnessed the unconditional love of the dog softening the hearts and spirits of these so-called hardened inmates. I walked into a cell that housed four men and four dogs and the level of peace and serenity in that small containment unit was absolutely surreal. I could not believe it—before my eyes were four men in blue prison jumpsuits sitting on their beds, and four mixed-breed dogs lying quietly beside them, housed in their crates. A prison is an extremely savage place to live, and here we had peace amongst chaos. What if we had trained these men to become Wolfkeepers *before* they entered the prison system? What if the Wolfkeeper Nation that I am proposing to be created was to provide funds to train at-risk youth to train the thousands of unwanted dogs that are put to death every year?

When I hear about children and adults fighting dogs, I wonder how and why they have gotten to the point where they have lost appreciation for the value of life of another living creature. This lost appreciation for the value and dignity of life carries over into human interactions as well. I think about the celebrities who risk their million-dollar careers over fighting dogs. When I consider people who abuse dogs in order to make money from puppy mills, I see them as people who have lowered their standards and values for pure profit. When I contemplate the dog food companies that create inferior products that have been known to be harmful to our dogs simply for financial gain, I don't think of faceless corporations—I picture men and women who have completely lost their connection to the spiritual things that set humans apart from other living creatures.

When I spent time at Animal Care and Control and witnessed all the dogs that were there because someone abused them, it infuriated and troubled me. Why would anyone abuse a puppy and, more importantly, how did they get to the point where they even were capable of such an act? Did similar abuse happen to them? Dogs will continue to be abused and tortured by these lost souls until a majority of Wolfkeepers take seriously the art of raising, training, and advancing their canine companions and motivating and teaching others to do so as well. When you look into the eyes of your dog, if you are treating it correctly, all you will see is unconditional love. Many of us have never experienced unconditional love like this from any other living creature. Healing our relationships to our beloved dogs is the starting point to healing ourselves and our country.

*   *   *   *   *

Five years ago I met a dog trainer from Israel, whom I was excited to meet because of her experience with the military canine group "K-9." However, when I encountered her for the first time I was amazed by the level of aggression and hostility she had towards Palestinians. I had never personally met anyone who shared this sentiment towards another group of people simply due to their ethnic background, so I found it disturbing and fascinating at the same time. I wondered how this person could work with dogs and harbor such a strong level of hate at the same time. She told me that I could never understand the things that she had seen or been through as she showed me her arm, which still contained pieces of shrapnel from a Palestinian bomb. I explained to her that working with me and my dogs would teach her to be gentler and kinder to other people and would change her perspective on her past situation. I knew this because prior to meeting her, I had met many gang members, prison inmates, drug addicts, and others who had changed as a result of becoming connected to their wolves.

One day as I was upstairs working with the dogs, something told me to go downstairs to check on my new student. I saw her walking towards an aggressive Akita that was tied to the wall, but she had forgotten that she was holding a Yorkie in her arm. As she approached the Akita to give it a correction for obsessively barking, the Akita grabbed the Yorkie, shook it like a rag doll and almost killed it. I pried the Akita's mouth open to rescue the Yorkie and was bitten by the Akita very badly in the process. My once angry-at-the-world student was crying uncontrollably as she held the bloody Yorkie in her arms. She looked up at me with the saddest eyes I've ever seen and asked me what she should do. I told her that she was going to be responsible for telling the owner what happened, paying for the vet bill, and for nursing this Yorkie back to health in her home. By the time she had completed all of these tasks, she had become a completely different person. She never again mentioned her hostility towards Palestinians, and just acted calmer in general from that day on.

I have witnessed people in situations like this showing more compassion for animals than they show their fellow humans. Sometimes it takes a wolf to turn us into a lamb, and I believe that this is why God has given us these creatures—to transform us back into the gentle souls we were when we came into this world.

CHAPTER 6
WORKING DOGS
IN CONDOS

It is imperative that we learn to not extinguish the spirit of our dogs, but to channel that spirit.

When a dog lives outside and is allowed to bark, run, jump, and just be a dog, they don't exhibit the behavioral problems of most urban dogs—separation anxiety, submission urination, or fear biting—because they are allowed to be truer to their genetic essence of being a wolf. It is essential to take your urban dog to the country or somewhere they can just run around freely, or take them to swim in a lake. A dog that is not allowed to occasionally run freely will become a broken wolf—a city dog with multitudes of behavioral problems. It is natural for a dog to mark its territory, but obviously people don't want their dogs urinating on their expensive furniture. Is the answer to strip our dogs of the ability to just be a dog?

When you place a breed such as the American Bulldog (formerly known as the Alabama White Dog)—a dog that was designed to hunt wild boar—into a high-rise condo, how can you not expect it to have a few behavioral issues? This kind of working dog wants to bite, run, and bark, but these are deemed unwanted behaviors in an urban dog. When dogs are forced to live in an unnatural environment where they cannot use what they were genetically developed to do, then I consider this training against their genetic essence. A German Shepherd not being allowed to guard or track or a Beagle not being allowed to hunt is considered training against their genetic essence. When animals go wild, it's only because we are trying to force them to be something other than what they were bred to do. A good example of this is circus animals living in captivity.

The dog is a descendent of the wolf, and we must respect that this distant cousin is still somewhere inside them, still containing the essence of the wolf. Our mission as Wolfkeepers is to harness and control the wolf essence in order to keep our family pets safe in the unnatural environments in which we have forced them to live. It is natural for my American Bulldog to want to be dog-aggressive, but I must use extreme obedience and other activities to channel that energy in a constructive manner.

If a Japanese Akita living in a condo grabs a loaf of bread, it's very natural for it to growl and bark if someone threatens to take it away. The ripping of the bread bag can be similar to the ripping of a rabbit to the dog. The dog's natural instincts dictate to the dog that it needs to protect from other predators the prey it has captured. Training at an early age is necessary because we must train against many different inherent genetic aspects of the dog. There is no difference to the dog between a loaf of bread or a rabbit—both are captured game. However, some 800,000 people every year see the manifestation of the failure to teach some dogs the difference between the two and train against their natural primal instincts. Therefore, the new urban dog is plagued with a multitude of various behavioral problems.

Most modern dogs will spend 90% of their lives inside of a house or apartment. We must make sure that our dogs have the highest level of training possible and receive the maximum amount of exercise on a regular basis in order to avoid developing unwanted behaviors. When dogs live outside, or at least spend a great deal of time outdoors, it heightens their senses of hearing and smell—all their senses, bringing them closer to being a wolf again. It is imperative that we learn to not extinguish the spirit of our dogs, but to channel that spirit.

CHAPTER 7
OLD SCHOOL
TRAINING

"Old School Training" was hitting a dog with a rolled-up piece of newspaper or pushing its nose into its own pee or poop in order to housebreak the dog.

"Old School Training" was hitting a dog with a rolled-up piece of newspaper or pushing its nose into its own pee or poop in order to housebreak the dog. For most dogs "sit" and "down" were enough commands to learn. There was no need to make a dog heel at every corner, because most dogs didn't go for walks through the neighborhood—they just ran around in their own backyards. This is before the days of the behavioral problems that would be exacerbated by dogs' sometimes pampered living conditions—doggie daycare, boarding facilities, dog parks, and the ability to bring your dog shopping with you at overpriced pet store chains.

The urban dog is currently faced with a barrage of new problems, because they are forced to live in condos and houses and spend long hours waiting for their masters to return home. The dog of 2009 is not my grandfather's dog, bought for $5 back in 1940. There are 68 million dogs in the U.S. with more than 68 million problems. How dogs are trained must keep up with the evolution of the pet industry. If not, the number of dogs destroyed due to bad behavior will continue to increase. The world needs more Wolfkeepers to keep these dogs safe in the world in which they are forced to live.

The complexities of owning a dog are often trivialized, so the intricacy of their behavior is not appreciated or understood. Even a Yorkie can have you in court saying, "Your Honor, he was always so good with kids! I don't know what happened!" Dogs don't just live in basements or strictly outside anymore; therefore, they have more opportunities to administer bites or act out as they are constantly being exposed to more intense environments. When working your dog bring it to the busiest corner in your city and

experience the challenges
of training your dog in
a chaotic environment,
because unless your dog
has been trained to be
indifferent to the highest
stimuli you are walking
around with a potential
lawsuit.

Alpha in <u>All</u> Aspects

Alpha starts in your head.
It is necessary for Wolf-
keepers to be in charge in
all aspects of their lives. If a family has out-of-control children,
then they probably also have an out-of-control dog. If people are
bullied at work or school by their peers, then they are probably
going to be bullied by their Rottweiler. We are sometimes afraid
or not knowledgeable enough to be Alpha, take charge of our
lives, and not allow ourselves to be submissive or a follower. If we
are afraid to be the leader when raising a dog, this will result in
raising a dog in a "Cupcake Household"—a household where,
consciously or unconsciously, the owner is afraid of his own dog;
if not actually afraid of the dog, he is afraid of what his dog is
capable of doing. Dogs view things very black or white—either
you're their leader or you're not. If you are not the leader of your
Cane Corso or Presa Canario, a lawsuit may be waiting for you
around the corner.

If you own a Pit Bull, you'd better be Alpha at work, at
home, *and* at play or one day that cute little puppy is going to put
your leadership skills to the test. Just an FYI—in a wolf pack the
weak leader is normally killed by the emerging Alpha wolf!

"Amores Perros"

"*Amores Perros*" (Spanish for "Love and Dogs", or "Love's a bitch")
means to me that the dog is the final manifestation of what's going

on in our lives. I realize now that when my mother was going through a divorce in 1978, our dogs were definitely displaying the negative energy of the household. I realize now why Rocky the Doberman was always barking, why Brach the Afghan was so docile, why Asia the Afghan was always trying to run away and why Channel the Poodle was always trying to bite. They were absorbing, embracing, and internalizing the nervous energy of a turbulent household, and that was displayed through excessive barking, passive-aggressive actions, and biting.

When I was four years old my mother asked me to put a sweater on her poodle and then walked out of the room, leaving me alone with the dog. His recognition of my fear enabled him to be that much more aggressive toward me. I attribute the loud voices and screaming and other disturbing things I saw happening in our family to the negative behaviors manifested in our animals.

Dogs residing in households where two people are constantly fighting sometimes suffer a seemingly accidental death, or simply run away. My theory is that the dog is such an emotional sponge that it can't handle high levels of emotional stress sometimes emitted by humans. Therefore, the dog takes its leave of them—one way or another.

Every Alpha wolf or pack leader will orchestrate the atmosphere of the den and the behavior of the wolves. Most of the time I can tell what kind of household the dog grew up in by just hanging out with it for a few hours. The majority of behavioral problems in dogs stem from their environment. Therefore, it is impossible to change the dog without changing their environment, especially if the environment is toxic. The dog becomes a barometer to reflect back to us how our lives are going. A dog is a very useful emotional gauge or soul thermometer. For example, aggressive human = aggressive dog, which bites a child. That human's aggression will be revealed in court during the lawsuit.

Remember when Barney, President Bush's Scottish Terrier, bit a journalist when he tried to pet the dog on national television? Maybe Barney overheard one too many conversations about going to war. Wolfkeepers will discover how to balance their own soul in the process of mastering the training of their dogs. Dog training is like a martial art that molds a person into a new being. I wish I could have worked with President Bush and taught him how to train Barney—maybe there would have been no Iraq War.

If a woman works from 6pm to 3am at a Wrigley Field sports bar and comes home covered with the layers of odors of human pheromones, alcohol, illegal drugs, and simply the stress of working there, her Beagle will internalize and manifest a response to her internalized emotions. This dog might become super-anxious, fearful of men, protective—especially at 3am, and show levels of separation anxiety, all due to what the owner brings home from work. We can change our culture by changing our dogs, because they will always let us know what we need to change about ourselves.

Very recently, my grandmother Bettye Williams Freeman died in the house that we shared. Two days beforehand my six dogs displayed phenomenal behaviors I had never seen in them before. Diesel barked excessively, as if there were a bitch in heat around; he urinated in the house; and he ate the cushions off the couch. My stress levels were high—the woman who helped raise me was dying before my eyes—and my dogs were revealing all my emotions. I told my Aunt Tammy that my dogs "are running hot." She asked what that meant, and I said that's when they are extremely agitated by something. Two days later my granny died. Before I walked into her room and discovered that she had passed away, my dogs had an eerie peace about them and a bone-chilling, subdued look in their eyes—especially contrasted to their behavior in the two days previous. This, to me, is *amores perros*.

Chapter 8
A Dog Is
Like a Gun

A dog can save your life if an intruder enters your home; but what if the intruder is your teenager's friend sneaking in for a late-night visit? Can you stop the bullet once it has left the barrel? If you cannot, you are waiting for a lawsuit or worse.

When your dog goes into fight mode or goes after prey, can you stop it from attacking the object of its attention? A dog can become an instant lawsuit because the owner does not have total control.

Recently, a woman decided it would be a great idea to own and raise a 200-lb.chimpanzee in her home, until one day it went berserk and ripped off her friend's eyes and nose. The primate had to be shot and killed by the police in order to stop the attack. Some people think that they can domesticate any animal of any species. However, no matter how many years of so-called domestication we impose upon the modern day canine, we will never completely strip them of their genetic wolf code. We must remember that at any given moment our so-called family pet can rip the eyes and nose off our neighbor's child.

I had a client whose Bullmastiff-mix knocked over a 5-year-old child—a cancer patient whose dad worked for the local police department. The owner was later sued for $160,000. All dogs need to have a certain level of control in order to make them safe in our urban environments. What makes a great protection dog is the ability to send the dog in for an attack and at the last moment command the dog to retreat back to the side of the master, and the dog obeys.

A family that I worked with had four unneutered male Labradors living together in a three-bedroom house. Not surprisingly, one of the males killed another during a fight over a bone. If we decide to put dogs in strenuous circumstances such as this, the level of training necessary to command dogs in all situations must be superb. A dog can save your life if an intruder enters your home; but what if the intruder is your teenager's friend sneaking into your house for a late-night visit? Can you stop the bullet once it has left the barrel? If you cannot, you are waiting for a lawsuit or worse.

Because we have stripped dogs of their natural packs, we have created dogs that develop cage rage. In addition, most dogs spend their entire lives eating dog food and never raw bones, so they never have the ability to relieve stress by chewing on hard substances. Therefore, without training, dogs become consumed with nervous energy and are walking time bombs just waiting to put their mouths on something. In addition, most urban dogs don't get enough regular exercise, so that contained energy adds to their cage aggression. (I consider the condo a cage for our dogs.) It's natural for a dog to want to bite, but we must channel that energy into a recreational outlet.

Dogs were originally put to use to protect us during wars, serve us in prisons, and guard us and our children; however, most dogs will never live as working dogs. The 800,000 dogs that critically injure humans every year are 800,000 dogs that were never trained to the fullest by their masters; many will meet a needle in their necks, all because the owner failed the dog.

CHAPTER 9
RESEARCH THE
TRAINER

Most people only contact a trainer when they run into problems they can't solve while training their dog. Find a trainer before you obtain your new pack member.

If a Wolfkeeper starts training their pup early, at about eight weeks of age, using many of the more harsh devices, such as choke collars and prong collars, can be avoided. Back in the old days all we used was a leather collar and a leather leash in order to train our dogs, and we had awesome results. When seeking out a professional dog trainer, it is crucial to know what training devices the trainer uses, and more important, understand and agree with why they use them. I do not believe it is proper to use an electric collar to shock a dog into submission, nor do I support the constant use of metal chains around a dog's neck.

Many of the pet store-chain dog trainers or people who have declared themselves dog trainers are not skilled at training dogs and are not trained to coach and teach the owners either. Don't let just anyone train the animal that's going to live in your pack for the next ten to 15 years. It is important to discern whether this person loves dogs or is in it just for the money. Always find out what their dog training lineage is—who taught them how to train dogs? If they have no lineage, then did they graduate from an accredited dog training school? Have they been studying dog training on their own for at least six to ten years before calling themselves a "professional"? Find out if the trainer has trained with other trainers and if so, for how long. There are many trainers who are not qualified to train a Yorkie suffering from separation anxiety, much less an aggressive Pit Bull Terrier. In addition, find out what kind of demonstration dog the trainer has and what kind of dogs they have trained in the past.

Always get references from other people before giving anyone money to train your dog. There are a lot of dog trainers, but very few great trainers/teachers. A dog trainer must be able to train the dog and the owner. The owner of the dog should feel thoroughly educated and prepared after interacting with a professional dog trainer.

Most people only contact a trainer when they run into problems they can't solve while training their dog. Find a trainer *before* you obtain your new pack member, and be sure that the trainer can help you understand how to prepare your yard and your house and which are the proper dog training tools and supplies to purchase. Find a person that doesn't mind dog hair all over their clothes or the smell of dog poop, and who's going to stick by you while you acclimate your dog to your world.

A great dog trainer is a teacher and trainer—someone who can make sure that the human completely understands how to train their dog. In order to join this fraternity of professional, private dog trainers, I spent many hours cleaning dog kennels and being the obedient grunt of my mentors. I learned from some of the greatest trainers on the planet and I realized that learning how to train a dog is an art, like learning a martial art. Once, I walked into a training facility and one of my mentors was actually inside a dog crate with a dog. I never did ask him why he did that; all I knew is that he meant serious business as he sat there in the crate with an aggressive German Shepherd.

One of the many characteristics that all my mentors shared was a vibrant, charismatic personality that calmed and demanded respect from all dogs. I would watch the way Jim walked in his yard around the dogs and they would avoid even bumping into him out of respect. My other mentor, Master Gypsy, could ignite the fire in a dog owner as he preached the importance of dog safety. The people from whom I learned are like Master Jedi—they are the last of a dying breed of professional dog trainers. I remember Jim telling me about a family that could not even get into their own house because their Rottweiler would not allow them to come in, and how he had to extract the dog from the house. I trained a Hurricane Katrina rescue named Mikey—a two-year-old American Bulldog that I had to feed through a muzzle for at least a week, because he tried to bite everyone at my facility. The art of training an aggressive dog, a dog that gets pleasure out of seeing you bleed, is an expressive art indeed.

I once trained a Korean Jindo that a little old grandma found and, for some strange reason, wanted to keep; this was one of the most aggressive dogs that I have ever encountered. The grandma's veterinarian called me and asked me if I would train the dog—they had it at their office and wanted to know if they could bring it over as soon as possible. I agreed and told them to drop it off and that my client manager, Kelly, would take care of everything. About 20 minutes later, I received a phone call from Kelly, screaming hysterically, demanding that I get back to the shop immediately. The transporter, terrified of the dog, had opened the door and just let the dog loose in the shop, slammed the door shut, and run off, and the dog was running around the shop, thankfully at least with a muzzle on. I got back to the shop and met one of my few canine nemeses—Rocky the Jindo. It took about three months to attempt to train Rocky; this is one of the few dogs I've attempted to train that I could not save, and that makes me sad even to this day. However, because of my experience with Rocky I have developed multitudes of training skills. Now, seven years later, I believe that it is very unlikely that I would meet a dog that I couldn't save. I have an entire series of bonding/relationship-building programs, doggie yoga, basic/advanced obedience programs, and mental challenge programs that I believe could save the worst dog on the planet.

I believe it's necessary to train a lot of aggressive dogs in order to be confident enough in your skills to consider yourself qualified to help someone prevent and/or dissipate aggression in a dog. I was hired to train a Cane Corso named Peaches that bit the owner's sister and a few other people. When the dog was dropped off she tried to bite me in the interview. The owner gave up on Peaches, but she is currently one of my personal pets—proof that any dog can be rehabilitated if the trainer has the knowledge, experience, and skills.

* * * * *

POPULAR TRAINING SERVICES

It is crucial for you to determine the best training program for your dog. The most widely used training programs are club training/group classes, private lessons, or doggie boot camp. The concept of using club training or group classes for a brand new dog is flawed. Unless the dog is owned by an experienced handler, club/group classes will be a waste of time and money. The totally green, inexperienced handler should take a couple of private lessons from a professional dog trainer prior to joining a club/group class. The group class should be used as a means to train your dog in a high-stimulus scenario. The experienced trainer will be able to work a green dog in this situation, but a green handler with a green dog is a recipe for disaster.

The new handler should visit a group class a few times before joining the group and interview the lead trainer before signing anything or parting with any money. Also, find out if the group class offers a certification program or testing program for the dogs after completion of the program.

Private lessons are great for dogs that have special behavioral problems or certain training needs that have to be addressed. Any dog that has aggression issues should be trained in a private setting. In addition, dogs that suffer from separation anxiety or are extremely hyperactive or puppies under 16 weeks of age should be trained in a private lesson. A person should train with a master trainer at their home, at a training facility, dog park, or other environments for dogs with severe behavioral problems.

DOGGIE BOOT CAMP

Doggie boot camp, where the dog lives with the trainer for two to three weeks at their training facility or home, is great for dogs with extreme aggression, extreme separation anxiety, or for owners who just don't have time to train their dog. Doggie boot camp works if the trainer actually takes the time to work with the dog every day, and is able to transfer the training techniques and knowledge over to the owner/handler.

When I first started training dogs professionally I used to keep six to ten dogs in my small two-bedroom apartment, which forced me to quickly learn how to control and manage a pack in a small setting. I learned what certain barks mean when dogs communicate to each other. Also, when observing dogs in a pack setting it becomes easy to determine how dogs establish pack order through play, barking, and fighting. I would strongly encourage the new Wolfkeeper to volunteer time at a kennel or shelter in order to observe dogs in a pack setting.

Most very aggressive dogs are trained in my doggie boot camp program. This is where I keep the dog for about 30 days and retrain all of their undesirable behaviors; then I return the dog to the owner and I train the owner. Dogs are shaped by their environment, and I have created a home environment that can and will reform the toughest and most obstinate dog.

*   *   *   *   *

Once a woman called me at 6 a.m., waking me up after a very late night. This was during a time when my dog training business was doing so well that I had purchased a BMW M5 and a custom van with my company's logos all over it. My skills were going to be put to the test after this phone call. The call was from a woman named Lisa who was calling from a heroin rehabilitation center somewhere in southern Illinois. She said that a counselor had given her my name and number and that she hoped I could help her. She told me that she had a Pit Bull named Ruby that was at her ex-husband's mother's house, and she asked me if I could get it out of the house before he returned home from prison after serving a sentence for drug trafficking. Even after a late night, that woke me up instantaneously! She explained to me that they had purchased the dog together, but then broke up—he went to prison and she went to rehab, and the dog had been living with his mother until Lisa was released from rehab. She had just found out that he was going to be released and would be home before she was, and she knew he would take the dog and she would never see it again.

I sat at the edge of my bed, thinking that there was no way I was going to any woman's mother-in-law's house to get a Pit Bull before her ex-husband comes home from prison. I can see it now: "Oh, excuse me sir, just picking up the dog like your ex-wife asked me to; don't mind me."

Lisa pleaded and cried until I finally caved in and asked her for the address. She gave me an address in Canaryville. Canaryville is a place where ten years ago, without a doubt, a black man walking down the street would find religion very fast and hopefully he could run even faster. There was no reason for anyone of color to ever just go "hang out" in Canaryville—even if that had changed, I never received the memo.

So, let me see, I am to go get a Pit Bull from an ex-con's mama's house in Canaryville, and the person who is commissioning this Kamikaze mission is in drug rehab. I took a deep breath, closed my eyes, said a prayer, and then agreed to do it. Then Lisa said, "Oh, yeah, one more thing; his mom has multiple sclerosis and you will have to pick her up from her friend's house and bring her to her house and help her put a collar on the dog." My brain was racing and I was doubting my sanity as I took down all her information and hung up the phone.

Later that day I went to pick up the mother-in-law from a rundown old house in Canaryville. I called from my cell phone once I was outside, as I had been instructed, and an elderly woman using a cane came slowly walking out of the house. I helped her into my car and she was very talkative and thanked me over and over, and said that she was glad I was picking up the dog, because she wasn't sure her son wanted to take care of it and he was coming home later that day. All I could think of was this guy was going to make it home early, or one of his friends was going to see me with his mom in his house, taking his dog, and then the day might take a really bad turn.

When we got to the mom's house she walked in first, and the Pit spotted me and aggressively charged the door, barking and snarling. The mom could barely get in and close the door, and I just about pushed her in the house and slammed the door to keep the dog from bolting out and attacking me. It must have really looked good—I was on the front porch peeking through a slightly cracked door at an angry, agitated Pit Bull not wearing a collar. I asked the mom if she could at least get the collar on and she said, "No, my MS is starting to kick in and get really bad, and my hands won't stop shaking."

I told her to take her time and just try to get the collar on the dog. If I had the collar on everything else would be OK. I stood on that porch for about 45 minutes coaching her through the door until she finally got the collar on the dog. She was almost in tears out of frustration and, at the same time, happiness at her success. Now all we need is the leash on the dog and then I can do my "Dogman" thing. She got the leash on, handed it to me through the door, and the rest is another book.

I have experienced hundreds of scenarios like this over the last seven years and have had thousands of deep, sad conversations about people's personal problems. Sometimes I have spent more time listening than training, and I realize now that teaching the human is the first step to successfully training a canine. I spent many hours on the phone and in person talking to Lisa about her Pit Bull and her ex-husband. I can sincerely say that that day taking that dog out of that house changed my life, and it changed Lisa's life also. She found someone who cared about her and her dog even though we had never met; and an elderly mom found someone who didn't care about race, because that day on the porch race didn't matter, and who should or shouldn't be in Canaryville didn't matter. I know deep in my heart that we need more people like me who can help dogs—and people—in this situation, and then we will have an army that can change the world.

CHAPTER 10
TRAINING
YOUR WOLF

Ultimately, when a dog hears any of our commands we want them to do that command perfectly and immediately; but this will only happen if the dog training and conditioning is consistent.

Every dog—no exceptions—should know basic obedience. When teaching a dog basic obedience be open to whatever technique best serves that particular dog. The only criterion that counts is whether the training methods used will hold up under *any and all* stimuli. My preferred method is using a leather collar and leather leash on dogs with no behavioral issues—that way I know that they are exhibiting the desired behaviors due to the training and not due to the implements used. Also, if a leather collar or leash breaks during training and the dog gets away and causes damage, it is much more beneficial to your case if you can show a snapped piece of leather, rather than a frayed piece of pretty pink nylon. If a dog has a below-average trainability aptitude then I will use a choke collar; and finally, if a dog is older and has multiple training problems I will use a training collar (often called a "prong" collar).

What we call "bad" behavior is often quite natural for a dog. However, we don't want them to have that particular behavior in the urban environments in which we have forced them to live. For example, a dog barking at the door if it hears an intruder on a desolate ranch in Bozeman, Montana would be exhibiting very desirable behavior. However, a dog barking at every little noise outside his owner's condo door is exhibiting very undesirable behavior. A dog living in Kenya exhibiting animal-aggression and protecting itself and its owners from wild boars is exhibiting desirable behavior, but a dog living in Chicago establishing physical dominance over another dog by attacking and killing it is exhibiting undesirable behavior. A dog lying beside you and defending you from intruders while you're in a sleeping bag in a tent by a campfire in Brazil is good, but a dog that's allowed to sleep on the bed and which bites the boyfriend when he stays over is bad. A hungry dog growling at a human or another animal and that is ready to attack while eating its food in a dark New York alley for survival purposes would be, while not necessarily a good thing, at least understandable, while a dog growling at a child who is eating her food in her highchair in the kitchen of a condo would be unacceptable.

For example, it's natural for Tina's Chihuahua Pancho to want to pee on the leg of her thousand-dollar oak table when he smells Fifi the Poodle next door, because he is marking his territory against other male dogs. If Pancho was in the wild his natural ability to mark his territory would be part of his survival. However, when living in a Michigan Avenue condo or a Beverly Hills mansion it's not acceptable for Pancho to raise his leg to mark his territory. This is where you will have to learn how to become a Wolfkeeper in order to teach Pancho how to control his natural genetic responses like marking, barking, biting, and growling. Therefore, we have developed basic obedience, advanced obedience, various dog competitions, and dog tricks to help the dog channel these impulses into a more desirable outlet.

As another example, it's natural for an Australian Cattle Dog or a Belgian Tervuren to want to bite at your ankles or nip your feet and hands—you own a herding dog in the middle of the city and it needs something to do! Therefore, your dog should be taught to push a cart or balance a ball on its nose.

As a Master Wolfkeeper, I consider it animal cruelty to own certain breeds and not use them for what they were designed and bred for, or to not train them to use their natural responses to do something else. If a German Shepherd puppy's natural instinct to protect, chew, and work is not allowed, but rather it is trapped in a small condo and scolded every time it barks or bites, you can push the dog to the point where it will run away, retaliate against its owner, retaliate against strangers, become dog-aggressive, become passive-aggressive, or just simply die inside. Humans and wolves aren't meant to be locked in these concrete jungles—we are supposed to be outside under God's sky. We were intended to feel the rain, experience the cold, touch the grass, and hear the wind. However, just like our dogs being caged in kennels all day or at doggie daycare, if we Wolfkeepers become unbalanced and spend too much time at our desks in our cubicles at work we will become unbalanced like our dogs. Then behavioral problems will be shared and exacerbated between owner and dog.

The relationship between Wolfkeeper and dog is very much poetic and constantly evolving, because we are always seeking balance in our own lives and controlling our natural desires to do certain things that God designed us to do, like living in the wild and experiencing all our wonderful, natural responses. This is why I believe the outdoor dogs of the 70s and 80s lived longer, because living outside heightened all their senses. When our senses are heightened we are more in tune with nature, because we feel and experience everything with sharpened clarity. We medicate dogs, children, and adults because it pains us to try to control our natural senses in these concrete jungles. The dog wants to run and be wild, just like you, but can't because of the social ramifications for both of you. Therefore, that energy must be channeled; otherwise both owner and dog will be unhappy and unbalanced because all their tendencies to be creatures of nature are suppressed.

Dog training should be viewed in the same way you view training a child. You're not going to be able to tell a two-year-old baby, "Come here," and expect her to respond right away, if at all. Puppies and dogs are similar in that they don't understand what you mean when you say, "Come"—they have to be conditioned and taught. If you show a baby some car keys or a colorful cell phone and say in a sing-song voice, "Come here, baby; look what I have," he might try to crawl his way to you. It's the same thing with a dog—if you use a happy voice and a treat and lightly pull on your dog's leash, the dog will soon associate that sound with the desired action.

If you were teaching a three-year-old toddler how to sit in a small chair and stay there, every time she got up, you would put her back until she realized she needed to stay seated. It's the same way with dogs—every time they break the sit position, I will use my hands and put them back into that position. They will learn through repetitive action from the handler/trainer.

Dog training is nothing more than just doing the same action over and over again until puppy or dog does that action before being touched. There is nothing natural about dog training for the canine, because "Down," in the dog's mind, means "Submit." We want the dog to "Down" because we need them to be in one place for an extended period of time. We must provide an incentive for the dog to down, so if we use a treat and lightly pull on the leash until the dog downs, we will get the dog to down through consistent repetitions of the same action.

You can think of dog training as computer programming— we have to place the same identical chip into the dog's mind to get the same consistent response. Ultimately, when a dog hears any of our commands we want them to do that command perfectly and immediately; but this will only happen if the dog training and conditioning is consistent. Just like mastering golf or any other sport, dog training is something that takes hours of practice for both the handler and the canine.

I hope you understand why I believe it is so important to train your dog and push it to the maximum limit, not only in order to survive, but to thrive in your world. All dogs are born with unconditional natural reflexes, and it's natural for them to exhibit certain behaviors. However, these reflexes don't necessarily fit into our environments; therefore they must be controlled and redirected. Basic and advanced obedience is necessary to stop dogs' natural desires to act on these reflexes.

Never leave any dog unattended outside, because anything can happen—no matter how secure you think your yard is. ... You will never know how much you love a dog until you lose it.

I WILL NOW EXPLAIN THE TECHNIQUES I EMPLOY AND WHY I BELIEVE THEY ARE NECESSARY IN ORDER TO TRAIN YOUR DOG.

The Training Triangle is my principle concept for teaching a dog house etiquette, or how to live successfully with humans. Depending on how quickly it learns, <u>the dog will be in one of three locations for the first two to three years of its life:</u> (i) underfoot, (ii) in its crate, or (iii) outside.

THE FIRST LOCATION—UNDERFOOT

The handler will keep the dog underfoot by leaving them on a light cat leash and placing their foot close to the buckle of the leash. This is where the dog will be when you're eating, watching television, on the phone, or on the computer. This is not teaching the dog "Down," but to submit. Remember, in the dog/wolf world the "Down" position means "Submit," and what we are asking the dog to do is to submit to our control. In addition to teaching the dog to submit, the handler is gaining passive Alpha points over the dog and teaching the dog to be comfortable with being by the side of the master. The goal is to get the dog to the point where it will stay by the side of the handler at all times without a leash. A puppy or dog will naturally mostly want to stay by your side, but the true objective is to get it to stay by your side under extreme distractions.

It is necessary to practice keeping your dog underfoot in various challenging environments so that the dog learns patience, regardless of the circumstances. In addition, when keeping the dog underfoot you are putting the dog in a situation where it cannot fail. If it is by the side of the master, then it is not able to destroy anything, urinate, defecate, bark, or whine. Don't shoot the dog;

just don't allow it to be in certain situations. This will also assist in the house-breaking because the puppy/dog won't have the opportunity to pee or poop while underfoot.

When raising a dog in a household they should not have the option to just roam around the house until they are completely off-leash trained. Most handlers will not keep their dogs on a leash in the house, therefore they increase the likelihood of the dog developing various behavioral problems; for example, barking at the door when it hears the doorbell, chewing on furniture, and/or having uncontrollable aggression issues.

The Second Location—In the Crate

The crate is a place for the dog to be safe—it is their home and their bedroom. When we provide a crate for our dog we are tapping into their genetic instinct for a den, like the ancient wolf. All wolves seek a den and place to eat, drink, and find refuge. The urban dog needs a den within your den. The kitchen, your bed, and the living room is *your* den and not theirs. If you cannot watch your dog put it away in the crate! A dog should be put in its crate so much that at some point in time it retreats to the crate on its own.

When you first start crating your dog you can put an old piece of clothing in the crate to comfort it with your smell. In addition, put the crate in a high traffic area, so the dog can become accustomed to quietly being in its crate under high stimuli. Also, the crate can be covered with a blanket in order to make it feel more like a wolf den. If you feed, give water, and allow the dog to sleep in its crate, it will not urinate or defecate in its den.

The Third Location—Outside, Supervised

Never leave any dog unattended outside, because anything can happen—no matter how secure you think your yard is. Treat your dog like a two-year-old baby who needs constant observation in order to stay safe. You will never know how much you love a dog until you lose it, so don't let your dog be stolen or hit by a car. Don't leave your dog unattended outside, **ever**. In addition, a dog should be supervised outside in order to correct them when they make errors in your yard, like digging, chewing, and obsessive barking.

Our dogs *want* to know the rules of the pack and den. In the wolf world, if one wolf approaches another wolf's food it will

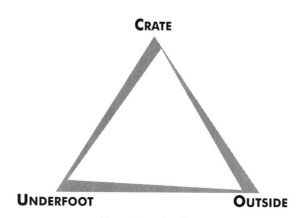

TRAINING TRIANGLE

CRATE

UNDERFOOT   OUTSIDE

HOME BASE 1—CRATE
—Food in crate
—Water in crate
—This is where your dog is if you're not supervising

HOME BASE 2—UNDERFOOT
—Leave a light leash or cat leash on your dog at all times
—Keep your foot on the leash:
    – When watching television
    – When on the phone
    – When on the computer
—If you are walking around your home keep the leash tied to your belt loop

HOME BASE 3—OUTSIDE
—Your dog should go outside to the same exact location to pee and poop
—The doggie only has 15 minutes to pee and poop
—Separate pee-and-poop time from play time

KEY NOTES
—When using the "Training Triangle" your dog is always in one of these three Home Base locations.
—The more disciplined you are with following the training triangle the quicker your dog will adapt to its environment.
—Dogs crave discipline!

growl, then snap. A mother dog will snap at her puppies if she doesn't want to nurse anymore. A dog will nip at another dog's legs to get them to move in certain directions. Dogs have dog fights in order to establish pack order and to show dominance. The best way to teach our dogs pack order and establishing and maintaining Alpha over them is by keeping a leash on them until they are completely off-leash trained.

"Off-leash trained" means the dog will do all of the following consistently in *any* environment without being told more than once: "Sit," "Down," "Stay," "Come," "Heel," and "No" (and/or "Zee"). In addition, a leash should be kept on the dog until they are completely house-trained. A dog should never be hit by a hand or any other object, because this will cause the dog to become hand-shy. Hand-shy dogs have the potential to bite someone who's reaching out to pet them, because they think they are going to get struck. If you don't leave a leash on your dog, you will surely hit them with your hand out of frustration.

A client of mine was over at her friend's house and saw his Pit Bull chewing on her shoe—she quickly hit the dog on the rump and the dog just as quickly put 20 stitches in her arm. Another client tried to get her Jack Russell Terrier off her bed by grabbing the dog by the collar, and the dog bit the owner on the hand. Still another client had a dog that bit the doggie daycare attendant when she tried to stop the dog from biting another dog—she pulled the dog by the collar, and the dog turned and bit the kennel attendant. Kennel attendants and pet professionals are bitten on a regular basis because they don't leave leash devices on dogs that don't belong to them. It's a show of Alpha to dogs to have a hand reach for them; but if you leave a leash on them you have a non-threatening way to correct them or remove them from a situation.

Also, when you leave a leash on your dog, you never have to chase them or move towards them aggressively. If you need to retrieve your dog, you can always move slowly to its leash and reel it in to you. This is why I consider the command "Come" an advanced command and not necessary initially for the dog or puppy in basic training, because this dog should never be more than the distance of the leash away from the handler in the first place. Therefore, for the first year of their life they are never in a situation where they need to "Come," because they are always close to their handler. This will eliminate 80% of unwanted behavior problems before they even have a chance to start.

My dogs never bark at the door or charge the door when strangers come in, because they never had the opportunity— I maintained leash control over them at all times for the first one to two years of their life. How long you make your dog wear a leash in the house will depend upon what your long-term plans or goals are for your dog. For example, a dog living in a household with eight children will require a higher level of obedience and must be able to perform under more challenging distractions, in comparison to the dog that will be living with a single person in a rural community. Take some time to make a ten- to 15-year life-plan for your dog. Figure out what potential changes in environment your dog will be required to undergo. Most shelter dogs become shelter dogs because the owners never created a game plan for the dog. Plan and train for the unexpected and your dog will be ready for anything.

CHAPTER 12
TEACHING
COMMANDS

Whenever you correct your dog, always show it praise after it stops the unwanted behavior. This way, you communicate to the dog, "Hey, nothing personal— just don't do that!"

"NO" COMMAND

For most dogs "No" is probably the first command they learn. However, we also want to teach a different word to use as "No." I use the command "Zee," because if there are 19 other dogs at the dog park and your dog is number 20, you want to be able to communicate directly to your dog if a dog fight breaks out—calmly telling him "Zee" while the other 19 dog owners are all screaming, "No, No, No!"

If starting with a puppy, in order to teach them the "No" command you should keep a light leash or a cat leash on them at least for the first year of their life, depending on how quickly they learn. Whenever the dog exhibits undesirable behavior—attempts to jump up on someone, chew on a shoe, chase the cat, bite someone—give the dog a quick jerk on the leash and say the command "No," and alternate it with "Zee." (This is like teaching a child "No" in two different languages.)

When teaching your dog "No" it is necessary to give the dog ample opportunities in a supervised environment to make errors and then to correct while the behavior is being exhibited. The best corrections are the unexpected corrections; so when your dog is trying to dig in the garbage, slowly and quietly walk up behind it, grab and jerk the leash, and firmly say, "No!" This way we develop a "No" checklist engraved into the dog's brain—things not to do when left alone in your house for eight hours. Don't give "mosquito" corrections, but when correcting your dog or puppy always swiftly and firmly jerk the leash as if you were pulling a small child away from fire. Also, whenever you make a correction always praise the dog after it stops the unwanted behavior. This way, you communicate to the dog, "Hey, nothing personal—just don't do that!"

TEACHING THE "CLIMB" AND "SIT"—A GOOD FOUNDATION

Teaching "Climb"

I like to teach puppies and dogs the "climb" command first; this helps them to develop focus and concentration. When teaching this command, place your dog behind a milk crate or a heavy-duty box, chair or stool of similar size; imagine invisible walls on both sides of the crate, and the dog has to come through the front door. Place your right foot at the left hand corner of the crate and your leash in your right hand and gently pull the dog forward and repeat the command "Climb." If the dog doesn't climb on the crate in five seconds abandon the mission and show the dog lots of praise for five seconds—then repeat the exercise.

The goal is not to force or place the dog on the crate, but to give the dog the option of eventually climbing on the crate on its own. This is a slow process, but it quickly develops focus and concentration and the beginning of a thinking dog. This is like doggie algebra for your pet, so show patience and take your time. The goal is to get the dog to climb on the milk crate by itself. Once the doggie has learned to climb onto the milk crate by itself, that is when I start teaching the doggie to "Sit" while on the crate.

Teaching "Sit"
When teaching the dog "Sit" the dog is always on the left-hand side of the handler. Historically, hunting dogs stood to the left of the handler because the rifle would project hot shells to the right and injure the dog. This tradition has never changed, whether for the "Sit" or the "Heel" commands. However, the dog should be able to perform properly on either the left or the right.

When I start teaching a dog the "Sit" command I like to only have a leather collar on it if possible. However, if the dog is showing greater-than-usual resistance I will use a choke collar or a training collar. Once your dog is on the crate, you can hold a small piece of hot dog close to its nose; slowly raise the hot dog over its head until its rump is descending to a down position; as its rump is descending use your left hand to press the rump completely into a down position. Repeat this exercise five times in a row with treats, and then do the exercise without treats; but this time place the leash in your right hand and pull up on the leash quickly and push down on the rump quickly and say "Sit." Practice this five times in a row and then go back to working the dog with treats and then back to working the dog in "compulsion mode" (no treats). When you work your dog with both treats and compulsion you will give them two reasons to complete the task requested.

To review, teach the dog "Climb," then "Sit," and then we will teach them "Watch."

The "Watch" Command
Once your doggie has mastered "Climb" and "Sit" it's time to teach the "Watch" command. While your dog is in a "Sit" position on its milk crate, stand right in front of it and place a piece of hot dog in your mouth. Mumble the word "Watch" three times and

then bend down and let your dog take the food from your mouth. Once your dog has mastered taking the food from your mouth while you're bending, stand straight and from this position start dropping the food from your mouth. If your dog misses the food as it is dropped, don't allow it to have the food—just quickly dispose of it if it hits the floor. Once the dog is at complete attention and waiting for you to drop food from your mouth, you must start weaning the dog off the food and teaching him "Watch" with your leash. Make your dog climb on the crate, then sit, and tell him to watch and every time he looks away, give him a quick jerk on his leash and make him watch you, the Master Wolfkeeper.

You must practice this around distractions so that the dog is enticed to look away; this way you can correct him every time he

looks away. This exercise should be continued until your dog's eyes are completely locked onto you whenever he hears the command "Watch."

Mastering "Down"
You must first understand that "Down" means "Submit" in the wolf world. Wolves and dogs "down" naturally to show submission to other animals. However, we want them to "Down" automatically for control purposes, such as leaving them in extended "Stays." Some dogs might completely resist the "Down" command because it challenges their genetic Alpha status. However, teaching a dog "Down" is one more way for you to establish yourself as the pack leader.

When teaching a dog "Down," make the dog climb on its crate, then "Sit," then "Watch," and then hold a piece of hot dog in front of its nose and slowly let your hand descend like a floating balloon until the dog goes into a "Down." If the dog breaks the "Sit," place them back into a "Sit" and repeat the "Down" exercise with food.

Once the dog has learned "Down" with treats, it's time to teach "Down" with compulsion only. Make the dog climb on its crate, then "Sit," then "Watch," and then lightly pull down on the leash as if your hand were a two pound weight. If your dog breaks its "Sit" when you pull down, place it back into "Sit" and repeat, pulling the leash and saying, "Down." If the dog doesn't "Down" in five seconds, abandon the mission, tell the dog "Off" and pull it off the crate and then repeat the entire sequence again.

The "Stay" Command

"Stay" means "don't move—claw if you have to, but hold your position." As the doggie is in a "Sit" on the crate, place the leash in your right hand and your left hand over their nose. Lightly and quickly tug on the leash about ten times with your right hand and repeat the word "Stay" with each tug as your left hand is covering the dog's nose. The ratio of a dog's sense of smell is 300 to our 1, and when you place your hand over the dog's nose you are overloading its senses with your Alpha pheromones. Sometimes the dog will fight you when you place your hand over its nose, but be patient and gentle and keeping working at it until there is zero resistance. In addition, lightly push down on the dog's nose while your right hand is tugging the leash forward and keep repeating the word "Stay."

Next, place your left hand over its eyes and again quickly tug on the leash about ten times with your right hand and repeat the word "Stay" with each tug. When you place your hand over the dog's eyes you are making the dog trust you by removing its visual cues, which develops the foundation for a concrete "Stay." Next, run your hand down the back of your dog very firmly all the way to the rump, like you were screwing its rump into the ground, and continue to tug the leash with the right hand and keep repeating the command "Stay." Now, again quickly tug on the leash about ten times with your right hand and pump and flash your open left hand at the dog while you repeat "Stay."

Finally, back up to the end of the leash as you're tugging the leash and repeating "Stay." At this point your dog should be fighting to stay on the milk crate as you tug on the leash. Do a quick, complete 360 degree circle around the dog, and if it jumps off the milk crate repeat the exercise until the dog stays, no matter what you are doing.

THE "HEEL" COMMAND

Why is it important that a dog walk by its master's side? What is the dog thinking when it spends its entire life at the end of that leash being pulled and restrained by two hands? A dog will develop collar and leash recognition if any one training device is used more than another; therefore, don't constantly just use a choke collar, training collar, or leather collar—it's necessary to practice training alternating all three implements.

The Instructions for Teaching "Heel"
Place the leash in your right hand, pull it around your front, and have your right hand positioned towards your back by your second belt loop on the right side. The left hand should not be on the leash at all. We will consider this the "strike hand." This technique will allow the dog to take advantage of the slack in the leash. Then, when we feel the dog forge ahead or pull forward, we will pull back quickly on the leash or strike backwards on the leash, then quickly remove the left hand from the leash. If we feel the dog lagging behind, we will quickly pull forward or strike up and then quickly release the left hand from the leash. If the dog pulls wide, we will pull in or strike in and then quickly release the left hand.

If a mother is holding her child's hand at a red light and she feels the child try to step off the curb she will quickly pull the child's hand back. We do the same thing as we combat our dogs' pulling on the leash. While the left is the strike hand, the right hand simply holds the leash near the second belt loop and doesn't move. If the dog doesn't see the right hand, then the right hand doesn't become part of the dog's visual conditioning and programming. The absence of the right hand forces the dog to strictly focus on the position of the left hand. We will consider the left hand as the stick shift or "heavy" (bad guy) until the dog has developed what I call "healthy paranoia."

It is a healthy paranoia when the dog looks up at the handler to determine in which direction he is going to strike the leash.

When using this training technique we want to give the dog ample opportunities to make an error, and when they take the opportunity we correct. If we constantly restrain the dog with both hands in the traditional "Heel" position, we will never teach the dog to consistently stay by our side at all times. A handler will eventually go to a one-handed leash position for some reason or another—to talk on his cell phone, to greet somebody, or to hold a beverage. The dog that has been trained to only respect *both* hands on the leash at all times will take advantage when he realizes that the handler is only using one hand, which is usually when a handler is wrenched off his feet on a patch of ice or dragged across the street when he tries to answer his cell 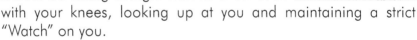 phone. This requires the handler to develop a new motor skill, where the left hand can react faster than the dog's action when they pull on the leash. Eventually, your dog will learn to walk patiently on a loose leash that's held only in the right hand.

When walking with your dog in "Heel," the dog should automatically go into a "Sit" when you stop. In addition, the dog should be sitting straight with its chest even with your knees, looking up at you and maintaining a strict "Watch" on you.

There are other heeling techniques that dogs need to learn, but if you can nail this basic heeling technique with your dog you will be ahead of the game.

"Interview Stance"
The "Interview Stance" refers to when you're walking with your dog, your head should be up, looking from side to side and behind you. Avoid looking at the dog when you are walking to see what he is doing, or you will encourage the dog to look around instead of at you. If you walk with your head up and look around and make

abrupt turns, your dog will learn to watch the movement of your head. For example, if someone broke into your home, you would want to get your dog on your side and slowly walk, keeping your distance from the intruder. You look around, or "interview" the room, and as a result your dog will watch you and look for your directions. In a dangerous situation like this you don't want your dog forging ahead and attacking or reacting without your direction.

Most dogs walk ahead and never look at their owners—in fact they hardly even glance at them or act like they know they're there. In addition, most handlers never look around when they are walking their dogs; they watch the dogs to see what *they're* going to do next or what *they're* watching! When you are walking/heeling your dog, you should move naturally with confidence like a pack leader.

Communicating While You're Training

It is imperative to talk to your dog constantly while training. This is connected to getting the dog to look up at you and to focus on your face. It is sometimes difficult for men handlers or handlers who are stage-shy to cheerlead and use high-pitched doggie-baby

talk with their dog. However, the mark of an excellent trainer is one who can talk to his dog while he's working with it. Everybody wants feedback when they are working hard for someone! A dog loves to hear "Good boy!" or "Good girl!" when working super-hard for the handler.

Most dog owners go nuts with explosive praise when they come home from work and see their doggie. This is the same enthusiastic, energetic emotion you should have in your voice when working your dog. If your dog is in la-la land and not paying attention to you, then you need to cheerlead more. Imagine making a dog-training video and you are the star of the show—will the show be exciting or will it be extremely boring and painful to watch?

In the dog world audible communication is important, so it's crucial that we create a vocabulary of sounds that the dog recognizes as "Hey, I'm doing a great job!" These sounds will become what your dog strives to hear as you walk in your downtown area with all the street noise. Then, the only thing that's making your dog watch you is your beautiful, energized cheerleading voice.

In addition to becoming comfortable with using your voice while training, you must also become comfortable working in a high stimulus situation. Quite often, the new dog trainer becomes the master of the kitchen or basement, and all the training and hard work falls apart when they come to the group class or go for a walk outside where all the yard dogs, rabbits, cats, and squirrels do their best to become distractions. When training your dog, practice around loud sounds and distractions. We want to create a dog that is accustomed to all types of visual, audible, and olfactory challenges in all environments. Therefore, take your dog downtown, by the train tracks, out to the country, to the dog park, to the pet store, and around loud crowds. The goal is to get the dog to the point where it is indifferent to all stimuli except you and the sound of your voice.

BALANCE

CHAPTER 13
VARIOUS LEVELS
OF TRAINING

In the process of challenging our dogs we challenge ourselves, and our dogs start to bring us to worlds that we never would have visited on our own.

Once you have accepted the concept of being a Wolfkeeper, your mission should be to push your dog to the maximum. Constantly train with your dog and get it certified in basic obedience classes. Once your dog has learned basic obedience, push yourself to teach your dog advanced obedience and some type of competition training.

The American Kennel Club has developed a test called the "Canine Good Citizen Certification," which is a nationally recognized certification that all dogs should achieve with their handlers. Dog training is so intricate and there are so many concepts and theories to cover that it would be impossible to discuss everything in one book and not overwhelm the new Wolfkeeper. However, all Wolfkeepers should work with as many dogs as possible in order to sharpen their dog training skills. It's a great idea to work at shelters and apprentice under a master trainer who has trained dogs professionally.

We should never consider a dog fully trained, because a new, challenging environment can potentially undermine your dog's training. This is why I believe that all dogs should be proof tested and certified by a trainer other than the one who trained the handler/dog team. We must constantly put pressure on the dog and look for new challenges until we can truly say that we have developed a dog that can thrive in just about any environment. In the process of challenging our dogs we challenge ourselves, and our dogs start to bring us to worlds that we never would have visited on our own.

I have demonstrated with my American Bulldog from the ghettos of Chicago to the farms of Minnesota, and have tested my level of controlled dog obedience in the prisons of Indiana. At the end of the day it's still a dog, and we never know what might make the loveable family pet attack the neighbor's five-year-old child. Because dogs can be so unpredictable, we must constantly place them in unpredictable situations. If not, the partially trained dog might have us in court paying a six-figure settlement to a grieving mom.

DIESEL WOWS THE LADIES!

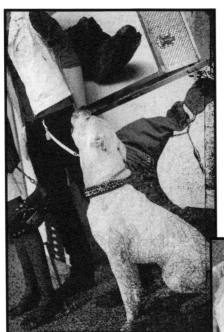

Diesel's wondering if these "people" are ever going to move!

PRIVATE LESSONS—
STARTING YOUR DOG OFF ON
THE RIGHT FOOT

**GROUP LESSONS—
PUTTING OBEDIENCE
LESSONS TO THE TEST**

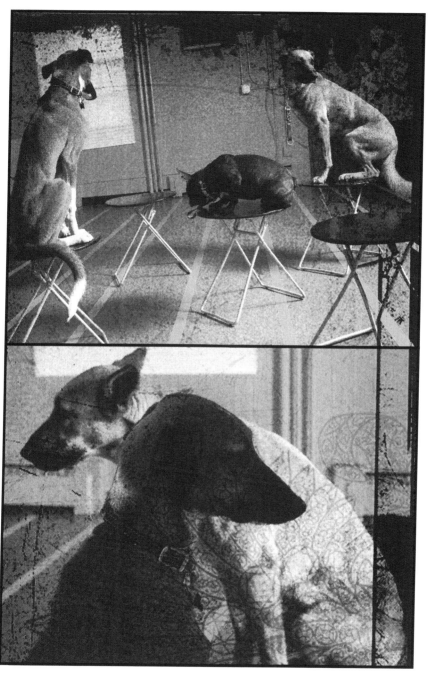

The beginning of a "thinking" dog
(thinking "Get me out of here!")

Diesel "supervises" Group Classes

Life's a beach!

"This isn't as easy as I make it look!"

"That fire hydrant thing is such a stereotype."

"um ... I think the light's about to change ..."

"This is a snap compared to sitting on a bike rack!"

Which paper did you want?

Shopping's such a bore!

CHAPTER 14
THE TEN
OBEDIENCE
COMMANDMENTS

In order for your doggie to survive ten years or more in your household, their level of obedience must surpass the amount of stimuli that will be imposed upon them during that time.

1. Keep a light leash or cat leash on your doggie for the first two weeks at all times. Keep doggie underfoot!

2. If you can't watch your doggie put him in his crate.

3. After feeding, take your doggie outside IMMEDIATELY.

4. Doggie should go outside at least three to five times per day for two weeks and then you can slowly reduce if necessary.

5. Give water and food inside the crate.

6. Practice obedience commands five times per day; each session should only be five to ten minutes long.

7. Be very strict for the first two weeks on all obedience commands.

8. Try to see to it that the doggie gets at least 30 minutes of cardio exercise per day.

9. Don't allow the doggie to run and explore the entire house.

10. Be Alpha and let other people know that your doggie is in training.

Change of Lifestyle

—Doggie does not eat in the kitchen!

—Doggie eats and drinks in crate!

—If you can't watch your doggie put him in his crate!

—Keep the crate located in a high traffic area!

—Keep a short leash on your doggie so you can make quick corrections!

—If you can't enforce corrections, don't give the doggie a command!

—30 minutes of cardio per day!

—PRACTICE, PRACTICE, PRACTICE. If you don't practice your commands, your doggie will get sloppy!

Continued Training/Group Classes

Group classes are an awesome way for the doggie who has graduated from doggie boot camp to put all the obedience commands to the test. In order for your doggie to survive ten years or more in your household, their level of obedience must surpass the amount of stimuli that will be imposed upon them during that time. In order to be fair to your doggie, you must continue to train and practice your commands.

CHAPTER 15 SPIRITUAL TRAINING AND HEALING

I have held dogs in my arms while they died, and they undeniably had a gentler and calmer transition due to the Reiki touch.

I am a First Degree Reiki Healer, and believe that all dogs benefit from being touched and comforted. I believe that doggie yoga, massage therapy, essential oils, and incense can help bring our urban wolves back into balance after years of living confined to condos, apartments, and houses. In addition, use of these types of methods and products helps make the bond between Wolfkeeper and dog that much stronger. I have seen miracles happen with the power of Reiki to heal injured dogs. In addition, I have held dogs in my arms while they died, and they undeniably had a gentler and calmer transition due to the Reiki touch.

DOGGIE YOGA

Doggie yoga can start at eight weeks of age and should be used as the first form of obedience training. Doggie yoga is also a great system to use when picking out a puppy. If the puppy shows too much resistance when implementing the yoga, then maybe that puppy is better suited to be a police dog than a family pet. Think of teaching obedience as doggie yoga, because ultimately the handler wants the dog to perform certain body positions on command.

After volunteering my time at Animal Care and Control and other various shelters for a few years, I realized that their temperament test did not really unearth the temperament of the dog being tested. Therefore, I developed my 12 Doggie Yoga maneuvers as a test of dogs' willingness to submit to certain positions imposed upon them. Doggie yoga also is therapeutic for the dog because it stretches joints and muscles that it cannot stretch on its own, and it strengthens the bond between master and dog through touch.

Over the years I have had clients who raised their dogs from puppyhood and have been able to do almost anything with their dogs, but sometimes have been bitten by their dogs during the process of learning doggie yoga. A handler should not find out he cannot get his dog on its side in the midst of a medical emergency. In addition, doggie yoga gets the dog comfortable with being handled, which in turn makes them less likely to bite. Can a handler manipulate his dog in any body position he wants? Surprisingly, often the answer is "NO!" There are many handlers—amateurs and professionals—who are afraid of their own dogs. Every year I get new clients whose dogs have bitten a mentally challenged person or a young child because they pulled the dogs' ears too hard. If these dogs had been accustomed to "The Ear Stretch Maneuver," the likelihood of them biting the unsuspecting victim would have been considerably lower.

The handler must be able to perform the doggie yoga in high stimuli environments. I was teaching a seminar class at the International Kennel Club, and I invited a Border Collie FlyBall group to join me on stage. I was not at all surprised when one of the flyball handlers was bitten by her dog when she tried to do "Puppy Scruff" with her. It can be dangerous for you and your children to live with an animal that you don't have complete control over.

Doggie yoga is also a great way to warm up your dog before taking it for a run. Just like any athlete, dogs need to warm up before beginning any physical activity. We've all seen dogs do their two big stretches before they start their day—"Down Dog Stretch" and "Up Dog Stretch."

A handler can also use doggie yoga as a means to calm their dog in a high-stress situation, such as being in a dog park or going to the vet's office. We want to create a dog that not only appears very calm, but acts calmly. I like to burn incense and use different essential oils, like tea tree and lavender, when doing yoga with my bulldogs. I have noticed while teaching group classes that some people who don't necessarily love working with their dogs on basic obedience enjoy getting on the floor to do some doggie yoga with them.

12 DOGGIE YOGA MANEUVERS

1.   *Puppy Praise:* Stand behind the dog and lift them up by their front paws, so they look like "Superdog." Now, wrap your right leg across the dog and gently stretch them back. (Repeat, crossing your left leg)

2.   *Puppy Cup:* Stand over or straddle dog and cup your hands under them as if you were praying, and lift dog up.

3.   _Puppy Rotate:_   Stand over dog and place your left arm under the dog's leg and hold it, and use your right hand to rotate the paw under the elbow in a circle.

4.   _Hands Over Eyes:_ Put dog into a sit position and squat over the dog, place hands over dog's eyes, pull hands back over eyes; now with your thumb and index finger massage the back of the dog's neck. Next, use your thumb and run it down the spine of the dog as if you were pushing a marble through a straw.

Can you tell Diesel enjoys this?

5.   _Ear Stretch:_ Straddle the dog and let the ears run through your hands as if you were milking a cow. As the dog gets used to this motion, apply some pressure, as if you were a small child who didn't know how hard to pull.

6.   _Wheelbarrow:_ Stand behind your dog and lift the dog up by its hind legs; place your thumb on the top of the thigh and the palm of the hand on the inner thigh—hold for a few seconds.

7.   _Paw Pressure:_ Squeeze the web between each paw and apply extreme pressure.

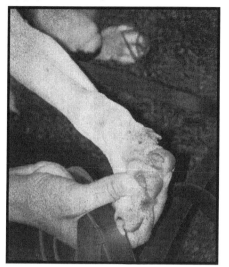

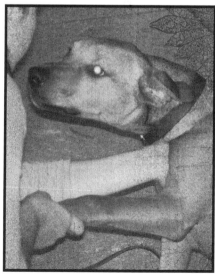

8.   _Lawnmower Stretch:_ Stand in front of the dog and place your left hand against their chest and their left paw in your right hand and gently PUSH and PULL, then SWITCH.

9.   *Mouth Stretch:* Open your dog's mouth and stretch gently, holding for a few seconds. Then gently clamp muzzle together and hold for a few seconds.

10.   *Ballerina:* Stand behind your dog and kneel on one knee, grab the nape of their neck and grasp their hind leg and stretch back, then push gently forward. Switch legs—repeat.

11.   *Reverse:* Place your dog on its side; stretch the top leg forward with your hand under their elbow and stretch back the hind leg they're laying on (big stretch).

12.   _Puppy Scruff:_ Stand over your dog, grab the scruff of the neck with both hands, and lift the dog.

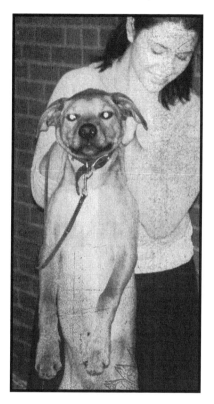

FEEDING YOUR WOLF

Raw Food
When I was growing up my great-grandmother, Queen Clarice Reed, would put table scraps in ice cream buckets and mix in a little dry dog food and feed it to our German Shepherds. I have no recollection of our dogs ever being sick. Also, I remember during the 1980s I saw a pack of alley dogs year 'round for about four years straight, and they survived simply off garbage or whatever they could forage. However, the garbage they ate was all human grade, unlike the modern dog food, which are inferior grade products that come from various unknown, often questionable sources. The dog food bag might state that it is chicken and brown rice, but it might be chicken that missed market date. When it says animal by-product meal, you don't know what part of what animal they have included to make that little piece of brown kibble.

When I was a dog food representative, I met a guy who worked on a road crew that sold road kill to manufacturing plants, which converted the carcasses to meal and then sold that to various dog food companies. There are companies that will purchase the carcasses from animal care and control and veterinarians' offices and also use those bodies as meal or as a protein source for dogs.

I will not tell you what to feed your dog, but I feel like I wouldn't be honest with you unless I told you how I feed my dogs. I like to feed my dogs raw turkey, raw chicken, and raw ground beef. I mix a little Flint River Ranch or other human grade kibble with the raw food as a supplement or I use a powdered supplement called Nupro. Feeding a dog straight dog food its entire life will cause it to become overweight and increase its chances of developing various diseases. My six-year-old American Bulldog, Diesel, has eaten a raw diet his entire life and he has never been to the vet for any problems. People always ask me how I got Diesel's body so toned and ripped, and I tell them it's from his being on a raw food diet. Whenever I meet a dog that is completely unbalanced, the first question I always ask is, "What is the dog eating?"

I don't confess to being a vegetarian or raw foodist, but I

try to incorporate aspects of both into my diet. Just like our dogs, we as humans should not consume all of the processed food that is available at grocery stores and restaurants. A Wolfkeeper should definitely be aware of their diets, so that they can keep up with their dogs. I believe that dogs can sense when we are out of shape and this is one of the ways that they gain Alpha status over certain handlers.

The goal of the dog owner is to push the dog to the maximum with regard to basic and advanced obedience.

The goal of the dog owner is to push the dog to the maximum with regard to basic and advanced obedience. The minimum amount of time it takes to completely train a dog (on- and off-leash) is 28 weeks. Note that to ensure successful completion, all obedience training must be tested by an outside non-biased dog trainer. The following is a list of what should be expected of each dog:

EVERY DOG SHOULD:

- have mastered on- and off-leash control
- be completely compliant being touched anywhere on the body by anyone
- be certified by dog trainers other than the one who conducted the training

<u>NO</u> DOG SHOULD:

- be aggressive to humans or other animals
- be easily excited by light and medium distraction
- be disobedient to its owner

TRAINING METHODS

Step 1:   Positive Reinforcement—Treat
Teach the dog to perform a command by using treats and praise.

Step 2:   Compulsion
Once the dog performs a command consistently with the use of a treat or praise, introduce slight compulsion. Slight compulsion is simply a tug/pull of the leash used to teach dog commands without treats or praise.

<u>Step 3:</u>   <u>Verbal</u>
Once the dog is performing the desired command consistently with slight compulsion, the next step is for the dog to master the command without any compulsion. Therefore, the dog must perform strictly on voice command.

TRAINING DEVICES

- 6-foot leather leash
- 6-foot cat leash
- leather collar
- choke collar
- training collar
- dog crate
- dehydrated hot dogs

Level 1:   White Training

All dogs that are 8 to 16 weeks of age must have mastered the following: "Sit," "Down," "Stay," and "Heel." In addition, they should be house-trained and well-socialized around other humans and dogs. Finally, all dogs trained by SSDT must master the 12 Doggie Yoga Maneuvers.

Benefits of Level 1—White Training – Puppy Class

• Basic obedience to aid with basic life scenarios that the dog will encounter
• House training that will make living with the dog easy and pleasant
• Necessary foundation to live a long life—ten-plus years without being relinquished

Level 2:   Yellow Training

All dogs that are 5 to 12 months old must be able to successfully complete the 10 American Kennel Club Canine Good Citizen Tests.

Benefits of Level 2—Yellow Training

• Completion of AKC-CGC training (dog is included in a national training registry)
• Certificate from the AKC-CGC recognizing such training and testing
• Proof of completion of an internationally recognized dog training test (helpful in potential legal cases that could be brought on against owner if/when an attack by the dog occurs)
• AKC-CGC pendant for dog

Level 3:   Red Training

All dogs that are 1 to 3 years old must be able to perform all obedience commands off-leash in a controlled environment.

Benefits of Level 3—Red Training
- Ability to attend family functions without being threatening or disruptive to humans or other animals
- Ability to visit pet stores, dog events, and dog socials without being disruptive
- Ability to perform commands without repetition or the use of compulsion
- Comfort and safety having small children around dog as verbal commands given from a distance of 15 to 20 feet will be followed

Level 4:   Black Training
All dogs that are 3 years or older should have mastered the following: off-leash control around light to heavy distractions in an outdoor setting. In addition, the dog should be indifferent to meeting humans or animals.

Benefits of Level 4—Black Training
- Full and balanced life
- Ability to compete in local and national dog obedience competitions
- Be an integral part of the SSDT Dog Training Masters Program (a group of dog owners that are committed to forming dog training clubs)
- Have the title of one of the nation's best-trained dogs (having completed over 28 weeks of training and being acknowledged by 4 outside trainers)
- Potential to motivate other people to train their dogs to a higher level with the hopes of reducing the number of dog attacks
- Partake in service work such as agility training, tracking, search and rescue, or therapy dog.

CHAPTER 17
SHOULD DOG TRAINING BE MANDATORY?

If laws are passed requiring the training of all dogs, most people would hesitate before spontaneously purchasing that English Mastiff puppy.

The Wolfkeeper's political agenda for 2009 is to lobby for laws enforcing mandatory dog training as an alternative to the breed ban laws that are regularly introduced. We must lobby for laws that require all dogs to pass a basic test and to be proofed and certified by a professional trainer in order to reduce the amount of dogs that critically injure humans every year. In addition, if laws are passed requiring the training of all dogs, most people would hesitate before spontaneously purchasing that English Mastiff puppy.

By requiring that all dogs be trained we will improve the status of our dogs in our urban communities. Also, if a national law was passed to train all 68 million dogs in the United States, there would be a need for hundreds of thousands of dog trainers, which would single-handedly stimulate the United States economy and generate billions of dollars through training services, licensing, veterinary care, and other dog services for the millions of newly responsible dog owners.

CURRENT STATE OF BREED SPECIFIC LEGISLATION IN CHICAGO, IL

My fellow Wolfkeepers, use this as template to find out which politicians in your area are trying to create breed banning laws or laws that are not fair to our dogs. Virginia Rugai, 19th Ward Alderwoman, has previously proposed a Pit Bull breed ban, and more recently has proposed a grandfathering approach to allow existing Chicago Pit Bulls to remain, but ban the import and breeding of new animals of certain breeds. The proposal advocates microchipping and muzzling existing Pit Bulls.

**PENDING SUPPORT FOR 2005 PROPOSED BREED-SPECIFIC
LEGISLATION (19 OUT OF 50 WARDS)**

Billy Ocasio (2nd), Leslie Hairston (5th), Anthony Beale (9th),
James Balcer (11th), George Cardenas (12th), Ed Burke (14th),
Thomas Murphy (18th), Virginia Rugai (19th), Daniel Solis (25th),
Ray Suarez (31st), Richard Mell (33rd), Carrie Austin (34th),
William Banks (36th), Emma Mitts (37th), Thomas Allen (38th),
Margaret Laurino (39th), Thomas Tunney (44th), Patrick Levar
(45th), Bernard Stone (50th)

The problem with this proposal: If the goal is to mitigate dog bite
attacks and save children from emergency room visits, this pro-
posal fails on its face.
* It will be ten to 15 years before there are no Pit Bulls left in
  the city, assuming Pit Bulls are the source of the problem.
  If any of the following premises are true, then this legislation
  will have only created a false sense of security.
* Pit bulls are not the only dogs that cause bite attacks.
  Within every breed, 15-25% of animals have failed industry
  temperament tests (source: American Temperament Test
  Society)
* "Pit Bull" is not an actual breed—it's an artificial media
  designation for a "vicious dog" which obscures what is the
  best way to respond to the problem. It's possible that public
  reaction towards Rottweilers and Pit Bulls is a media-cre-
  ated problem. Sample issue: How do you assess a mixed
  breed dog that may have some Pit Bull heritage?
* Breed-Specific Legislation has been proven to not work in
  other cities' implementations—dog bite frequencies are
  identical. The only benefit of BSL is that it allows the legis-
  lator to demonstrate to the public that he/she took action
  to supposedly solve a crisis.

ALTERNATE PROPOSALS
* Mandate professional-grade dog training for Illinois dog

owners based not on specific breeds, but based on passing mandatory individual dog temperament tests. Temperament tests may be administered by a decentralized network of dog trainers, veterinarians, and shelters, but should adhere to a single state standard.

- A standard for acceptable dog temperament will be established by an accredited industry body. Chicago has strong leadership with the CAPTA council of dog trainers. The AKC has created the Good Canine Citizen temperament test used as a temperament standard. The SAFER™ testing methodology designed by the Urbana-based ASPCA Animal Behavior Center is a scientifically based method in use by animal shelters today.

- Enable the enforcement of this mandate through a state certified tracking system, which would be constructed and operated by private-sector funding. Private incentive mechanisms will ensure data quality is maintained. The tracking system will maintain records of training history in a permanent centralized location which Illinois government agencies will be able to access.

- A dog that has been involved with one unprovoked bite, or labeled as "Dangerous" by the standards of IL House Bill 4238, should require mandatory training until dog has achieved a satisfactory temperament certification result, as designated by an industry board (strategy proposed by State Rep. Mike Tryon).

- Dog-bite incidents will be recorded and correlated to dog-training histories to determine the effectiveness of individual dog-training business operations.

- Measure results over time. If mandated temperament testing and training are not making an impact on ER statistics, then proceed with Breed Specific Legislation with less public opposition because all other alternatives have been tried and tested.

DIFFERENTIATION FROM PREVIOUS DOG-RELATED PUBLIC SAFETY LEGISLATIONS

- Proposed IL state legislation: HB4212, HB4213, SB1790
- Passed IL state legislation: HB4238, HB2946, HB 4711
- These proposed and recently passed legislations ban "risky" dogs or primarily increase penalties as their strategies to enact changed behavior (more responsible dog ownership). These laws increase punishments for offenses, but run the risk of being completely ineffective in making communities safer. Few dog owners are even aware of the recently passed laws and will not take responsible, preventative action.
- A mandatory dog training law will not only measurably improve the safety of communities, reduce property damage, reduce medical claims, and save lives, but also generate significant revenues by delivering a registration enforcement mechanism, and increased business income taxes from dog training service providers.

NET CHICAGO, IL BENEFITS

- Estimated avoidance of 4,416 dog-bite-related ER visits (mostly children)
- Potential new "training registration or temperament certification" fee revenues (200,000 dogs @ $30 = $6M) Higher targets if reaching 876,000 dogs.
- Higher rates of collecting dog registration revenues, enforceable by a registration system. The statistic of Cook County's history of collecting dog registration fees for all dogs in the county is unknown.
- Avoidance of $12M in annual dog-bite related economic damages.

NET ILLINOIS COMMUNITY BENEFITS—IF IMPLEMENTED AT STATE LEVEL, PER YEAR

- Estimated savings of $50M in total economic damages

- Estimated savings of $16.5M in insurance claims
- Estimated avoidance of 18,400 emergency room visits

NET IL GOVERNMENT REVENUE BENEFITS—IF IMPLEMENTED AT STATE LEVEL, PER YEAR

- $31.5M in increased IL state tax revenues from increased dog training business incomes
- $18.0M in registration revenues now collectable due to tracking mechanisms
- Unestimable revenues from out-of-state dog owners shipping animals to Illinois due to higher certification standards and industry reputation.

Key figures used in statistics
- United States dog population: 73 million.
- Illinois dog population: 3.65 million.
- Chicago dog population: 876,000.
- United States annually suffers $1B in total economic damages from dog bites.
- Illinois proportionally suffers $50M in damages. (Illinois' 12.5M population is 5% of U.S. population.)
- Chicago suffers $12M in annual dog-bite related economic damages. (Chicago population of 2.8M is 1.2% of U.S. population.
- National insurance property damage annual claims from dog bites is $330M (source: Insurance Information Institute). Illinois proportion is $16.5M. Chicago proportion of annual insured damage claims is $4M.
- National injury statistic is 368,000 people sent to emergency rooms each year from dog bites (source: CDC). Illinois proportion is 18,400 people. Chicago proportion of annual dog-related ER visits is 4,416 people.
- Assumption that 60% of Illinois' dogs require training due to temperament test failures—only allow A grade temperaments to be exempt, because damages are so severe.
- Assumption that Illinois is only receiving about 20% of reg-

istration revenues possible due to lack of tracking mechanism.

- Average of $300 net profit before taxes for an individual dog training client.

PUBLIC OPINION RESEARCH

The Illinois Institute of Technology conducted an opinion poll at the 2006 Chicagoland Family Pet Expo, which had 300 exhibitors and thousands of pet enthusiast attendees. Survey responders' demographics: 75% owned dogs, 91% were general public and not industry service providers. The average respondent was in the mid-40s, and about a third were accompanied by children. The poll sought to measure:

1. Public sentiment around the responsibility of owners to train their pets
2. Public awareness of national dog bite injury statistics
3. Public support for dog breed banning laws and mandatory dog training laws as solutions to dog bite statistics

 - 94% of respondents were unaware of the extent of dog bite injuries (According to the Centers for Disease Control, there are 5 million dog bites per year, 1 million needing medical attention; 1,000 children sent to the emergency room each day, 15 to 20 fatalities. (Each incident costs $16,600 on average, $1B in total economic damages to the U.S. economy.)
 - 92% of respondents answered that the dog bite injury statistics constituted a "very serious" or "serious" issue. A full 59% had switched to "very serious"/"serious" from "moderately serious"/"not serious" when educated about the statistics.
 - 63% of respondents still opposed a dog breed banning law even after exposure to the bite injury statistics.

- 41% of the survey pool said they would definitely support a mandatory dog training law, and 28% said they might support a mandatory dog training law under certain conditions.
- 100% of the respondents felt that dog owners had a responsibility to train their dogs.
- Overall, the survey indicated that this dog-owner segment of the population was very opposed to Breed Specific Legislation involving breed bans, and would, under certain conditions, support a mandatory dog training law. This study, if warranted, can be expanded to cover a larger demographic outside the dog enthusiast community.

| CHAPTER 18 BREED-SPECIFIC LEGISLATION | *The American Kennel Club does not recognize the dog breed that current Breed-Specific Legislation most commonly targets—the Pit Bull Terrier.* |

BREED SPECIFIC LEGISLATION—A SOLUTION THAT IS PART OF THE PROBLEM

I talk about breed banning a lot because I think that the concept of dangerous dogs is unfair to the dogs themselves. We must realize that due to the millions of unqualified dog owners and pet professionals around the world, some of our canines have become dangerous. Therefore, I have included researched information on breed banning to implore the 45 million dog owners in this country and around the world to fight breed banning and encourage their congressmen and state representatives to fight for mandatory dog training laws.

Breed Specific Legislation ("BSL") prohibits individuals from owning specific dog breeds, or places restrictions on individuals that choose to own specific breeds.[1] Jurisdictions typically enact BSL in response to a highly publicized dog attack by targeting the specific dog breed involved. For example, the Pit Bull-focused BSL in *Vanater v. Village of South Point, et al.*, resulted from media reports regarding Pit Bull Terrier attacks in a neighboring city.[2] Additionally, the Pit Bull-focused BSL in *Garcia, et al. v. The Village of Tijeras* resulted from an attack, just two months prior to its enactment, in which a Pit Bull Terrier mauled a nine-year-old girl.[3]

Notably, the American Kennel Club ("AKC") does not recognize the dog breed that current BSL most commonly targets—the Pit Bull Terrier.[4] The dog breed that the public has come to recognize as the Pit Bull Terrier is actually a combination of different types of Bull Terriers.[5] As a result, Pit Bull Terriers often have different characteristics that are common in other types of dogs.[6] This confusion regarding the Pit Bull Terrier and its defining characteristics has proven to be the source of much controversy surrounding BSL.

Contrary to popular belief, Pit Bull Terriers are not the only dog breed subject to BSL. In fact, states either ban or restrict seventy-five (75) different dog breeds in North America. These breeds range from the 14- to 18-pound Pug[7], to the 150-pound Neapolitan Mastiff,[8] to the classic companion dog—the Airedale Terrier.[9,10] The wide variety of BSL-targeted breeds is indicative of the suspect history of BSL. The targeted dog breeds have changed over the years, depending on the way that the media portrays and vilifies them.[11] For example, the Pit Bull Terrier and Rottweiler are currently the focus of most BSL discussions, but two decades ago, few people expressed concern over such breeds.[12] Instead, public attention surrounded the Doberman Pinscher.[13] Unfortunately, this cycle has made miniscule, if any, improvements to the dog attack issues that most legislatures hoped BSL would cure. Unfortunately, this cycle of BSL merely exacerbates the problem because studies indicate that irresponsible or abusive individuals often seek out BSL-targeted dogs, which increases the likelihood of a dog attack.[14]

Local municipalities within a state are typically the branches responsible for enacting, or choosing not to enact, BSL in accordance with that state's general animal control statute. Thirty-seven states currently have municipalities with active BSL.[15] Fortunately, however, municipalities in 14 states have also repealed BSL.[16] This chapter provides a thorough analysis of BSL by first explaining the constitutional grounds on which it stands. Although it continues to surprise some, BSL is generally a constitutional method that state and local governments can apply to address a dog bite issue within a community. Despite its constitutionality, however, BSL is an ineffective method for controlling dog bites. In fact, several highly reputed organizations actively oppose BSL. Finally, this chapter suggests alternatives to BSL for addressing the dog bite problem.

*   *   *   *   *

CONSTITUTIONALITY

"Can they do that? I should be able to handle my dog, my property the way that I want." Although there have been several challenges to the constitutionality of BSL and other regulations that limit dog ownership, the answer is unequivocally "yes." Challengers to BSL typically assert the following five arguments: (1) BSL is beyond the states' regulatory authority; (2) BSL violates constitutional due process rights; (3) BSL statutes are unconstitutionally vague; (4) BSL violates constitutional equal protection rights; and (5) BSL constitutes an unconstitutional taking of private property without just compensation. Successfully pursuing any of these seemingly legitimate arguments becomes an insurmountable hurdle since BSL's constitutionality is subject to the regulation-friendly 'reasonableness test.'[17] A reasonableness test applies because municipalities typically defend BSL as being a regulation that is necessary for the health and safety of the community.[18] According to the reasonableness test, legislatures need only establish that BSL has a "rational connection with the promotion and protection of public safety."[19]

Police Power

Courts clearly and consistently hold that BSL is within a state's police power to regulate because it is a public health and safety regulation.[20] A state's police power is its authority to regulate private property within its borders for the benefit of the public health, safety, and welfare.[21] The Tenth Amendment of the United States Constitution guarantees such power to all of the states.[22] Additionally, once a Court classifies a regulation as one for the public health, safety, and welfare, it becomes significantly more difficult for individuals to challenge the constitutionality of such regulation because Courts award public health and safety regulations "a strong presumption of constitutionality."[23] Therefore, Courts may hold that a BSL is constitutional because it is a regulation for the public health, safety, and welfare, even though they would not uphold a similar regulation enacted for a different purpose.

In *Sentell*, the United States Supreme Court outlined a state's police power to regulate dogs for the first time.[24] The *Sentell* Court upheld a statute prohibiting a dog owner from collecting civil damages for the killing of her female Newfoundland because she failed to comply with local dog registration and taxation ordinances.[25] In so holding, the Court stated,

> It is true that under the Fourteenth Amendment no State can deprive a person of his life, liberty or property without due process of law, but in determining what is due process of law we are bound to consider the nature of the property, the necessity of its sacrifice, and the extent to which it has heretofore been regarded as within the police power. So far as the property is inoffensive or harmless, it can only be condemned or destroyed by legal proceedings, with due notice to the owner; but so far as it is dangerous to the safety or health of the community, due process of law may authorize its summary destruction.[26]

Notably, the female Newfoundland involved in *Sentell* did not show any signs of viciousness, nor had she shown any such signs in the past.[27] In fact, she was a valuable purebred Newfoundland that her owners listed on the AKC's stud registry, and she was used for breeding purposes.[28]

According to the holding in *Sentell*, states have constitutional authority, through their police power, to regulate dogs, regardless of an individual animal's history or propensity to cause harm. This holding, although not specifically addressing BSL, laid the foundation for future BSL-related decisions. First, it provides that states have the authority to regulate dogs more extensively than other examples of personal property. Second, it protects BSL against Fourteenth Amendment challenges because the *Sentell* dog was subject to regulation despite the lack of any finding or evidence of viciousness. Third, the animal's value is an insignificant variable—even the most well-trained, well-bred examples of a dog breed are subject to possible destruction. Accordingly, a state is free to impose regulations upon entire dog breeds without any case specific application or researched logic, so long as the state can claim that such regulation affects the public health and welfare.

Additionally, in *Vanater*, the Court expressly disagreed with the plaintiff's argument that a state exceeded its police power by prohibiting Pit Bull Terrier ownership based on media stereotypes.[29] States must balance the property rights of an individual dog owner with its duty to provide for the public safety.[30] Since dog ownership is "not considered one of the cherished rights which the Court must carefully protect,"[31] a state's finding that Pit Bull Terriers pose a unique threat to the community is sufficient to justify the deprivation of an individual dog owner's property rights.[32] The Court therefore held that the *Vanater* municipality justifiably determined that Pit Bull Terriers posed a unique threat because of their allegedly "exceptional aggression, athleticism, strength, viciousness and unpredictability which are unique to the breed," among other things.[33]

DUE PROCESS

The Fourteenth Amendment of the United States Constitution created the due process guarantee by prohibiting the states from depriving any person of "life, liberty, or property without due process of law."[34] This guarantee encompasses all of the protections that are "implicit in the concept of ordered liberty."[35] One such protection is the defendant's opportunity to defend herself against any claims made against her.[36] In the context of BSL, this amounts to dog owners' ability to challenge a municipality's classification of their dog as a prohibited breed. Courts have consistently held that this protection does not extend to guarantee a dog owner's ability to challenge whether the legislature should have targeted a specific dog breed.

Commonly, a state regulates the manner in which authorities handle vicious dogs, while delegating the responsibility of defining a "vicious dog" to local jurisdictions or municipalities. When local jurisdictions define a "vicious dog" to include all members of a specific dog breed, BSL challengers often confront such ordinances as conflicting with the state's instruction to limit their regulation to "vicious dogs." In *Bess*, for example, the Court held that a local ordinance defining a "vicious dog" to include all Pit Bull Terriers was consistent with state regulation authorizing the confinement or destruction of dogs that a court determines as "vicious."[37] The local jurisdiction was justified in determining that Pit Bull Terriers were intrinsically vicious and a detriment to the public welfare because of their "inherent characteristics of strength, viciousness, aggression, and unpredictability."[38] Although the state's regulation provided for a specific procedure in which a dog owner could defend against a complaint that his dog was "vicious," this was not inconsistent with a BSL that labeled an entire dog breed as "inherently vicious."[39] The Court found this irregularity excusable because dog owners charged with violating the BSL could defend a court's classification of the dog as a Pit Bull Terrier by showing evidence, such as a veterinary certification that the dog was not a Pit Bull Terrier.[40]

Thus, according to *Bess*, a due process claim against BSL has nothing to do with determining whether an individual dog is vicious, or that it poses a threat to the public health and safety. Rather, a due process claim against BSL is only concerned with whether the ordinance affords an individual the opportunity to challenge whether a dog sufficiently falls within the prohibited dog breed. Courts need not engage in a case-by-case determination of whether an individual dog is itself "vicious."

Vagueness

Legislation is a violation of the Fourteenth Amendment's due process guarantee if it is so vague that it does not inform a person of ordinary intelligence of the specific activity prohibited.[41] "Because the ownership of a dog does not implicate fundamental rights such as speech or association, the ordinance should be upheld unless the dog owners are able to establish that the ordinance is unconstitutional on its face and incapable of any valid application."[42] The constitution does not require legislative acts to be mathematically certain or supportable by scientific evidence.[43] Therefore, a BSL is not unconstitutionally vague even if authorities cannot enforce it with mathematical certainty.[44] Legislation is only unconstitutionally vague if it fails to provide citizens with any acceptable standard of conduct.[45] Lastly, even though the statute does not contain a description of the prohibited dog breed, such description is readily available to dog owners through the United Kennel Club ("UKC") and AKC standards for the Staffordshire Bull Terrier.[46] BSL opponents further challenge BSL as unconstitutionally vague because the statute lacks a description of the breed's physical characteristics, and that such physical characteristics are even questionable because the AKC does not recognize the Pit Bull Terrier as a dog breed. Given the widely known reputation of the Pit Bull Terrier, Courts are reluctant to find even the most general description vague.

In *Vanater*, the Court upheld BSL with a very specific description of the prohibited dog breed. The BSL in *Vanater* prohibited ownership of any dog fitting the following description:

> [. . .] [A]ny Staffordshire Bull Terrier or American Staffordshire Terrier breed of dog, or any mixed breed of dog which contains, as an element of its breeding the breed of Staffordshire Bull Terrier or American Staffordshire Terrier as to be identifiable as partially of the breed of Staffordshire Bull Terrier or American Staffordshire Terrier by a qualified veterinarian duly licensed in the State [. . .].[47]

This was not vague because a reasonable person could easily refer to a dictionary, dog book or guide, or AKC standards for Staffordshire Bull Terriers and American Staffordshire Terriers to determine whether the statute applied to an individual dog.[48] The Courts have also upheld several generic dog breed descriptions. For example, the Court in *Garcia* approved an incredibly generic description of the prohibited dog breed.[49] The BSL at issue there merely prohibited residents from "own[ing] or possess[ing] [. . .] any dog of the breed known as American Pit Bull Terrier."[50] This description is notably generic because the AKC does not recognize any breed as an "American Pit Bull Terrier," and because it fails to reference mixed breeds or give a description of the defining physical characteristics.[51] Nonetheless, the Court held that the BSL was not vague because witnesses testified at trial that they could easily recognize a Pit Bull Terrier by its physical characteristics.[52] Additionally, the Court in *Dog Fanciers, Inc.* explicitly rejected the plaintiff's argument that the BSL was unconstitutionally vague because it did not provide a physical description of the prohibited dog breed, and thus permitted inexperienced and unknowledgeable law enforcement personnel to enforce it arbitrarily.[53] The *Dog Fanciers* Court upheld the BSL at issue there because it provided dog owners with some protection against such arbitrary enforcement by permitting them to challenge their dog's classification as a prohibited breed.[54]

Equal Protection
BSL opponents commonly assert that BSL is a violation of the Fourteenth Amendment's equal protection guarantee. In general, this argument asserts that BSL discriminates against citizens owning a dog with the physical characteristics of the prohibited dog breed, in favor of citizens who own a dog that does not have the physical characteristics of the prohibited dog breed. Because dog ownership is not a suspect class such as race or sex, legislation regarding dog ownership may discriminate so long as such discrimination is rationally related to a legitimate government interest.[55] Courts typically uphold BSL's level of discrimination when faced with evidence that a dog attack occurred involving the prohibited breed.[56] Such evidence indicates that the BSL is rationally related to the public health and safety.[57]

Under-Inclusiveness
BSL opponents commonly challenge BSL as being under-inclusive. Legislation is under-inclusive if it does not address all of the facets of the problem that the legislature enacted it to address.[58] In the context of BSL, where the municipalities enacted it to address a dog bite problem, the Courts have held that it is acceptable for munic-

ipalities to address the dog bite problem by addressing only a small percentage of it at a time through BSL. Again, the fact that municipalities typically defend BSL as being a regulation for the public health and safety plays an important role in this determination. The plaintiffs in *Garcia* argued that the BSL violated their equal protection rights because it was under-inclusive.[59] They argued, "[A]n ordinance banning only one breed of dog rather than all breeds, pure and mixed, bears no rational relationship to a legitimate governmental purpose."[60] The Court rejected this argument on the grounds that a governing body may address problems gradually, countering each threat as it occurs, as opposed to attempting to tackle the entire problem at once.[61] It is therefore unnecessary for a governing body to address the potential threats that all dog breeds pose to the community.[62] Accordingly, a governing body does not violate an individual's due process rights through BSL even though such ordinance is under-inclusive.

Over-Inclusiveness

A few BSL opponents have unsuccessfully asserted that BSL is unconstitutional because it is over-inclusive. The over-inclusive doctrine prohibits a state from making laws that punish constitutionally protected or innocent conduct.[63] This concept applies to BSL because if municipalities rationalize BSL by claiming that it addresses the dog bite problem, then BSL punishes owners that are innocent because it punishes dogs that have never bitten or displayed any signs of aggression. The Courts have refused to thoroughly examine this issue, however, because the over-inclusive doctrine applies only to conduct protected by the First Amendment of the United States Constitution.[64] The First Amendment of the United States Constitution does not so protect dog ownership.[65]

EFFECT

Does It Help?

Several well-respected and widely known organizations disapprove of BSL. For example, the AKC "strongly supports and actively promotes a wide range of programs to educate the public about responsible breeding practices and the responsibilities of dog ownership" as an alternative to BSL.[66] Additionally the American Veterinary Medical Association ("AVMA") has gone beyond merely expressing disapproval of BSL, to forming the Task Force on Canine Aggression and Human-Canine Interactions (the "Task Force") to assist communities in researching and formulating effective dog prevention plans.[67] According to the Task Force, BSL is nothing more than an ineffective knee-jerk response to the dog bite problem for five reasons.[68]

First, some communities justify their BSL on dog bite statistics that are inherently flawed.[69] Municipalities often fail to account for the fact that almost half of dog bite victims are children younger than 12 years old.[70] This is important because it reflects the idea that the victim's behavior plays a role in dog bites.[71] "[A] dog's tendency to bite depends on at least five interacting factors: heredity, early experience, later socialization and training, health (medical and behavioral), and victim behavior."[72] The media, through its depictions of a specific dog breed, is partially responsible for the role that an individual assumes when confronted with such a breed. Media depictions of Pit Bull Terriers have resulted in the view that they are "an abomination or disturbance in the natural order—an unacceptable threat to the perceived security and stability of the entire community and a violation of the almost sacred image of the dog as an amiable cultural hero."[73] This stigma causes individuals unfamiliar with the breed to react to a Pit Bull Terrier's presence poorly, such as by displaying fear or quickly leaving its presence.[74] These are both examples of inappropriate behavior that may increase the likelihood of an incident.[75]

Second, dog bite statistics record all dog bites as if they involved a purebred dog, which is often not the case.[76] Mixed breeds are often involved in dog bites, which lead to the use of guesswork to categorize a dog—whose exact breed is unknown—into predetermined categories.[77] Regardless of whether the description of the prohibited dog breed is specific or general, the difficulty in identifying mixed breed animals makes all BSL vague, although apparently not by constitutional standards. This poses significant problems to BSL's legitimacy because even animal experts incorrectly categorize dog breeds from time to time.[78] For example, it is relatively common to mistake a Boxer mixed-breed dog with a Pit Bull Terrier mixed-breed dog.[79]

Third, dog bite statistics are inaccurate because they do not record all dog bites that occur, but rather, only those dog bites that require medical attention.[80] Common sense indicates that larger dog breeds, such as a Pit Bull Terrier, have the physical ability to do more damage than smaller dog breeds.[81] Accordingly, even though people interpret dog bite statistics to demonstrate that larger dogs are more dangerous than smaller dogs, this is not the case—smaller dogs are not less likely to be dangerous, it is just less likely that a smaller dog will inflict enough damage to require medical attention.[82]

Fourth, community officials do not know the number of any given breed in a community.[83] This is true even if the community requires owners to register their dogs, because it is common for people to disobey such ordinances.[84] Accordingly, dog bite statistics fail to demonstrate the true proportion of any dog breed within the community that is involved in a dog bite incident.[85] For example, it is common for individuals to interpret an annual dog bite statistic showing that one dog bite involved Dog Breed A, and three dog bites involved Dog Breed B, to mean that Dog Breed B is more prone to dog attacks than Dog Breed A and, therefore, more dangerous. However, this would only be an accurate interpretation of the statistics if there were the same number of Dog Breed A and Dog Breed B in the population. If there are only three Dog Breed As in the population, but 30 Dog Breed Bs in the population, then 33% of the Dog Breed As attacked, while only 10% of the Dog Breed Bs attacked. Looking at the statistics this way, by including all of the relevant information, they indicate the opposite of what they initially seemed to show—that Dog Breed A is more prone to dog attacks than Dog Breed B and is therefore more dangerous. Because of this misconception, it is highly significant that community officials are often unaware of the total numbers of a given dog breed in a community.

Fifth, a dog's aggressive tendencies are not solely a product of its breed.[86] Several factors play a role in a particular dog's tendency to bite, such as:

(1)   early socialization, or lack thereof, of the dog to people;

(2)   sound obedience training for recognition of where he or she "fits" with regard to dominance and people, or mistraining for fighting or increased aggression;

(3)   genetic makeup, including breed and strains within a breed;

(4)   quality of care and supervision by the owner;

(5)   current levels of socialization of the dog with his or her family;

(6)   behavior of the victim; and

(7)   whether the dog has been spayed or neutered.[87]

BSL is ineffective because it fails to address any of these factors.

ALTERNATIVES

How do we address the dog bite problem?

The AVMA's Plan

For those currently facing the need to address a dog bite issue, the AVMA has proposed a plan for dog bite prevention that consists of five phases.[88] The AVMA stresses that anyone can facilitate dog bite prevention—from a group of concerned citizens to a government committee.[89] Phase One of the AVMA's plan involves determining whether any other groups have already invested resources into dog bite prevention.[90] This prevents the interested group from needlessly redoing any work that other groups have already completed.[91] Second, an interested group should establish a solid infrastructure that consists of the following parts:

(1)   a program coordinator responsible for collecting data, complaints, and concerns from the community;

(2)   animal control agencies that enforce local ordinances and protect the public health;

(3)   preventative measures including leash laws and licensing and vaccination requirements; and

(4)   post-bite measures, including investigative agents who explore dog bites, requirements for the quarantine of a dog who has bitten to ensure that it does not exhibit signs of rabies, and specific legislation defining a "dangerous dog" and awarding Court the authority to adjudicate a dog as "dangerous."[92]

Third, the interested group should encourage certain individuals, such as animal control agencies or health care professionals, to report dog bites to a central state agency.[93] Fourth, the interested group should educate the community regarding ways in which they can proactively prevent dog bites.[94] Lastly, the interested group can only achieve effective dog bite prevention by publicizing their efforts to the public through the media.[95]

OTHER ALTERNATIVES TO BSL

Dangerous Dog Laws

A "dangerous dog law" is a law that identifies unacceptable behavior on the part of a dog and its owners (meaning owners, harborers, keepers, and custodians); establishes remedies of various sorts; and authorizes third parties to take action to control the dog and its owner.[96] Thirty-two states currently have jurisdictions with dangerous dog laws.[97] Dangerous dog laws are more acceptable and effective than BSL for several reasons. First, dangerous dog laws only affect dogs that have already exhibited aggressive behavior. Accordingly, dangerous dog laws directly address the dog bite problem by only focusing on animals that are most likely to cause damage. Furthermore, dangerous dog laws are not over-inclusive because they do not punish innocent animals or their owners. Second, dangerous dog laws put the onus on the dog owner rather than the dog. This is effective because studies indicate that a dog's environment plays a role in their aggression level.[98] Third, dangerous dog laws are not restricted to any specific dog breed. This removes the ambiguity involved with BSL in determining a dog's correct breed. Fourth, dangerous dog laws recognize that all dogs can be a potential threat, regardless of breed. Fifth, dangerous dog laws do not exacerbate the dog bite problem by encouraging the public's fear of particular dog breeds.

California currently has a dangerous dog law in place.[99] This law has several safeguards to prevent the punishment of an innocent animal. First, it allows an action against the owner of a dog only after such dog has bitten a human being on at least two separate occasions.[100] This limits the statute's reach to dogs with aggressive tendencies. Second, the law allows authorities to consider the "conditions of the treatment or confinement" before issuing a final order.[101] After such consideration, the statute contemplates removing the animal from its area as opposed to destroying it.[102] Again, this demonstrates an understanding that a dog's environment is an important factor contributing to its temperament.[103] Furthermore, the California statute contemplates additional damages if a court finds that an owner trained the dog to fight, attack, or bite.[104] This effectively places the responsibility for a dog's inappropriate behavior on the dog owner and prevents improper training.

Irresponsible Dog Owner Laws

An "irresponsible dog owner" law is intended to identify and penalize chronically irresponsible dog owners."[105] Although no jurisdictions currently have such laws in place, dangerous dog owner laws could be an effective means of addressing the dog bite problem for the same reasons as dangerous dog laws. Additionally, dangerous dog owner laws may be more effective than dangerous dog laws in impressing upon dog owners the importance of proper care and treatment of dogs. For example, a dangerous dog owner law could punish behavior such as losing a dog or failing to control a dog in a public location, despite whether the dog caused any harm. This focuses solely on the dog owner's behavior and proactively prevents situations in which the dog is able to cause damage.

Obedience Training and Behavior Modification

Sound obedience training is an important factor that contributes to a dog's temperament.[106] As such, states could present owners of dogs that they would otherwise categorize as "dangerous" pursuant to a "dangerous dog law" with the option of attending obedience training and behavior modification courses as a form of retribution. Despite the fact that no jurisdictions have enacted such an ordinance, this would be a positive instrument to use in conjunction with dangerous dog laws. Instead of simply giving up on a "dangerous dog" this law recognizes that adequate dog training can tame aggressive behavior. For example, in a recent case in which authorities rescued numerous dogs that were bred and trained for the sole purpose of performing as fighting dogs, 47 out of the 51 dogs rescued were successfully retrained, rehabilitated, and sent to different civilian homes.[107] This example demonstrates that obedience training and behavior modification are useful and effective tools for taming dogs with aggressive tendencies.

Not-for-Profit Participation
Many not-for-profit organizations, such as the Humane Society and the AKC, already actively participate in programs that address the need for proper socialization of dogs and education of the public.[108] The AKC, for example, has promoted their Canine Good Citizenship Program ("CGC") since 1989.[109] Through this program, AKC representatives evaluate dogs and their owners on two different levels—one that stresses responsible pet ownership for owners and another that stresses basic good manners for dogs.[110] Cities and municipalities should strive to play a greater role within such organizations. They can do so by sponsoring events in which representatives from the different organizations educate the public, or at which dog owners can attend and receive CGC testing. This is a proactive way for cities and municipalities to address the dog bite problem by educating the public about the proper care of dogs before attacks occur.

CONCLUSION

BSL is essentially a knee-jerk and ineffective response to dog bites. Jurisdictions typically enact BSL based on inherently flawed statistics that do not accurately depict the true landscape of dog bites. Although BSL is constitutional, numerous studies indicate that it has little effect on the sole reason for its existence—decreasing dog bites. BSL is ineffective because it does not directly address dog bites or possible issues regarding a particular dog's aggressive temperament, such as a particular dog's training and environment. As such, alternatives to BSL should strive to make up for such shortcomings by directly addressing such issues. Several jurisdictions have already acknowledged BSL's ineffectiveness by repealing BSL and attempting to focus more resources on such alternatives.

NOTES

1   Hussain, Safia Gary, Note: Attacking the Dog-Bite Epidemic: Why BSL Won't Solve the Dangerous-Dog Dilemma, Fordham Law Review, April, 2006.
2   171 F. Supp. 1236, 1239 (S.Dist. Ohio 1989).
3   108 N.M. 116, 117, 767 P.2d 355 (App. N.M. 1988).
4   www.akc.org/breeds/breeds_h.cfm.
5   www.dogbreedinfo.com/americanpitbull.htm.
6   Id.
7   www.akc.org.
8   Id.
9   www.dogbreedinfo.com.
10   www.savealife.com.
11   www.hsus.org/pets/issues_affecting_our_pets/dangerous_dogs.html.
12   Id.
13   Id.
14   Id.
15   www.rott-n-chatter.com/rottweilers/laws/breedspecific.html.
16   Id.
17   Vanater, 717 F. Supp. 1236, 1242 (1989) (citing Keller v. Johnson, 425 U.S. 238, 247, 47 L.Ed. 2d 708, 96 S.Ct. 1440 (1976); Nebbia v. New York, 291 U.S. 502, 537, 78 L.Ed. 940, 54 S.Ct. 505 (1934)).
18   Id.
19   Id.
20   Vanater, 717 F. Supp. 1236, 1242 (1989).
21   Vanater, 717 F. Supp. at 1241 (citing Stone v. Mississippi, 101 U.S. 814, 818, 25 L. Ed. 1079 (1880); Jacobson v. Massachusetts, 197 U.S. 11, 25, 49 L.Ed. 643, 25 S. Ct. 358 (1905); Porter v. City of Oberlin, 1 Ohio St. 2d 143, 30 Ohio Op. 2d 491, 205 N.E.2d 363 (1965)).
22   Id.
23   Id. (citing Jackman v. Court of Common Pleas, 9 Ohio St. 2d 159, 224 N.E.2d 906, 38 Ohio Op. 2d 404 (1967; McGowan v. Maryland, 366 U.S. 420, 6 L.Ed. 2d 393, 81 S.Ct. 1101 (1961)).
24   166 U.S. 698 (S.Ct. 1897).
25   Id.
26   Id. at 705.
27   Id.
28   Id. at 700.
29   717 F. Supp. at 1244 (1989).

30 *Id.* at 1243.
31 *Id.* (citing *Sentell*, 155 U.S. at 704.)
32 *Id.*
33 *Id.*
34 Fourteenth Amendment, United States Constitution
35 *Danforth v. Minnesota*, 128 S.Ct. 1029, 1035, 169 L.Ed.2d 859 (S.Ct. 2008) (citing *Palko v. Connecticut*, 302 U.S. 319, 325, 58 S.Ct. 149, 82 L.Ed. 288 (1937)).
36 *Philip Morris USA v. Williams*, 549 U.S. 346, 354, 127 S.Ct. 1057, 166 L.Ed.2d 940 (S.Ct. 2007) (citing *Lindsey v. Normet*, 405 U.S. 56, 66, 92 S.Ct. 862, 31 L.Ed.2d 36 (1972)).
37 210 S.W.3d 177 (Ct. App. Ky. 2006).
38 *Id.* at 182 (citing *Garcia*, 108 N.M. 116, 120 – 21 (1988)).
39 *Id.*
40 *Id.* at 180 – 181.
41 *The Colorado Dog Fanciers, Inc., et al. v. The City and County of Denver, et al.*, 820 P.2d 644, 651, 1991 Colo. LEXIS 788 (S.Ct. Col. 1991) (citing *American Dog Owners Association v. Dade County*, 728 F. Supp. 1533, 1539 (S.D. Fla. 1989)).
42 *Id.* (citing *Hoffman Estates v. Flipside*, 455 U.S. 489, 71 L.Ed. 2d 362, 102 S.Ct. 1186 (1982)).
43 *Id.* at 650.
44 *Id.*
45 *Id.*
46 *Id.* at 652.
47 *Vanater*, 717 F. Supp. at 1249 (1989).
48 *Id.* at 1244.
49 108 N.M. 116 (1988).
50 *Id.* at 117.
51 *Id.* at 118.
52 *Id.* at 119.
53 820 P.2d 644, 650 (1991).
54 *Id.* at 644.
55 *Dog Fanciers*, 820 P.2d at 652 (1991) (citing *Kelley v. Johnson*, 425 U.S. 238, 247, 47 L. Ed. 2d 708, 96 S.Ct. 1440 (1976); *Austin v. Litvak*, 682 P.2d 41, 49 (Colo. 1984)).
56 *Id.*
57 *Id.*
58 *Zauderer v. Office of Disciplinary Counsel of the Supreme Court of Ohio*, 471 U.S. 626, 651, 105 S.Ct. 2265, 85 L.Ed.2d 652 (S.Ct. 1985).
59 108 N.M. at 121 (1988).
60 *Id.*
61 *Id.*
62 *Id.*
63 *The State of Ohio v. Robinson*, 44 Ohio App. 3d 128, 133, 541 N.E.2d 1092 (12th Dist 1989) (citing *Broadrick v. Oklahoma*, 413 U.S. 601 (1973)).
64 *Id.* (citing *Dandridge v. Williams*, 397 U.S. 471 (1970)).
65 *Id.*
66 American Kennel Club, Canine Legislation Position Statements, October 2008.
67 A Community Approach to Dog Bite Prevention, Journal of the American Veterinary Medical Association, Volume 218, No. 11, June 1, 2001, Page 1733.
68 *Id.*
69 *Id.*
70 *Id.*
71 *Id.*
72 *Id.* (citing Wright, J.C., *Canine Aggression toward people: bite scenarios and prevention*, Veterinary Clinic of North America Small Animal Practice, 1991, Pages 299 – 314).

73   *Managing the Stigma of Outlaw Breeds: A Case Study of Pit Bull Owners*, Tufts Center for Animals and Public Policy, Society and Animals Journal of Human-Animal Studies, Volume 8, Number 1 (2000).
74   *Id.*
75   *Id.*
76   *Id.*
77   *A Community Approach to Dog Bite Prevention.*
78   www.dogplay.com/articles/myarticles/pitbull.html#en6.
79   *Id.*
80   *A Community Approach to Dog Bite Prevention.*
81   *Id.*
82   *Id.*
83   *Id.*
84   *Id.*
85   *Id.*
86   www.hsus.org/pets/issues_affecting_our_pets/dangerous_dogs.html.
87   *Id.*
88   *A Community Approach to Dog Bite Prevention* at 1734 – 1735.
89   *Id.*
90   *Id.* at 1734.
91   *Id.*
92   *Id.* at 1735 – 1737
93   *Id.* at 1738.
94   *Id.* at 1739.
95   *Id.* at 1743.
96   www.dogbitelaw.com/pages/model_laws.html.
97   www.doglaw.hugpug.com/doglaw_090.html.
98   www.hsus.org/pets/issues_affecting_our_pets_/dangerous_dogs.html.
99   *Cal Civ Code § 3342.5 (2008).*
100   *Id.*
101   *Id.*
102   *Id.*
103   www.hsus.org/pets/issues_affecting_our_pets_/dangerous_dogs.html.
104   *Cal Civ Code § 3342.5 (2008).*
105   www.dogbitelaw.com/pages/model _laws.html.
106   www.hsus.org/pets/issues_affecting_our_pets/dangerous_dogs.html.
107   www.si.printthis.clickability.com/pt/cpt?action=cpt&title-what+happened+to+michael+vicks=dogs.
108   www.hsus.org/about_us.
109   www.akc.org/events/cgc/program.cfm.
110   *Id.*

APPENDICES

Test your knowledge by answering questions on canine training, nutrition and health; fill out and mail in a Behavior Fact Sheet and get a personalized response from Toriano about how to deal with your dog's behavioral challenges; and find a helpful 14-day training journal for you to copy and fill out as you train your wolf.

APPENDIX A

TRAINING QUESTIONS

1.   What is compulsion training?
2.   What is positive reinforcement training?
3.   What is clicker training?
4.   For what type of animal was clicker training first used?
5.   How are clicker training and electronic collar training similar?
6.   What is the proper name for a prong collar?
7.   What are three of the toughest breeds to train?
8.   What does "prey drive" mean?
9.   What does "food drive" mean?
10. What does "play drive" mean?
11. What should you do if a dog has no drive?
12. How should a training collar be properly fitted on the neck?
13. Why is it important to have a dry erase board while training?
14. What are the three components of the Training Triangle?
15. At what age should a dog start agility?
16. Name seven of the 12 Doggie Yoga Maneuvers.
17. Why do we use a leather leash and collar only?
18. Why should we always have some type of leash device on our dog?
19. At what age and level is a dog considered fully trained?
20. What does Doggie Yoga help accomplish?
21. Should you train a dog until it is tired?
22. Why is it important to take off choke or training collars before putting dogs in crates?
23. What does "under your foot" mean in regards to training?
24. Why do we stress crate training a dog?
25. Why is agility work helpful for dogs?

APPENDIX B
Nutrition Questions

1. What's the best kind of diet for a dog and why?
2. Do dogs have long or short intestines?
3. What should you do if your dog has diarrhea?
4. Can a dog eat raw meat and be healthy?
5. Why do some dogs eat their own feces?
6. Why is the protein content in dog food so important?
7. Why do dogs sometimes eat grass?
8. What is the difference between adult dog food and puppy dog food?
9. Why do puppies have to go out so soon after eating or drinking?
10. Why is "free-feeding" your dog incorrect?
11. Can overfeeding your dog be harmful? Why or why not?
12. Can too much water be harmful for your dog? Why or why not?
13. Is it dangerous for dogs to chew on raw bones from the butcher?

APPENDIX C

Health Questions

1. What is another name for kennel cough and what are its effects on a dog?
2. Distemper tends to cause what disorder in dogs?
3. How can rabies be prevented?
4. How is rabies usually transmitted?
5. Vaccinations can be given by injection and which other form?
6. How often should a dog's toenails be clipped?
7. What are the 4 main signs of an ear infection in a dog?
8. What is mange?
9. What is conjunctivitis?
10. What can cause excess coat loss on a dog?
11. How often should a dog be bathed?
12. Why is it important to clip a dog's nails?
13. How old should puppies be when weaned from their mother?
14. How many eyelids does a dog have?
15. What is the dog's most acute sense?
16. From which two main locations does a dog sweat?
17. Where are a dog's hackles?
18. When performing canine CPR, do you breathe into the mouth or into the nose?
19. When feeling for a pulse on a dog, do you feel for the artery in the neck or the hind leg?

APPENDIX D

BEHAVIOR FACT SHEET

Owner Name: _____

Address: _____

_____ Owner Marital Status: ___

Owner Phone (optional): _____

Dog's Name: _____ Age: ____ Sex: ___

Breed: _____

Behavior Challenges:

    ___ Dog Aggressive—Bites

    ___ Human Aggressive—Bites

    ___ Barks

    ___ Jumps Up

    ___ Play-Bites

    ___ Fearful of Dogs

    ___ Fearful of People

    ___ Potential Runaway

    ___ Pees and Poops in Crate

    ___ Destructive/Unruly

What have you done to correct these problems? _____

_____

_____

_____

_____

Where does the dog sleep? _____

_____

_____

_____

_____

At what age was the dog spayed or neutered? _____

Dog's reactions to "corrections" _____

_____

_____

_____

_____

Age obtained: _____ From where? _____

_____

_____

_____

_____

Reason you bought a dog: _____

_____

_____

_____

_____

House training method: _____

_____

_____

_____

_____

Has the dog ever been hit? Yes or No _____

Where, by whom, and for what reasons? _____

_____

_____

_____

_____

What games are played with the dog? _____

_____

_____

_____

How does the dog react to strangers? _____

_____

_____

_____

_____

Has the dog bitten anyone (broken skin)? Yes or No _____

How many times? _____Under what circumstances? _____

_____

_____

_____

_____

Dog's diet (main meal): _____

_____

How often? _____

Treats? _____
How often? _____

_____

Fill out this form and mail to:

> Toriano Sanzone
> 910 W. Van Buren St.
> Chicago, IL 60607

Toriano will review your answers and formulate a customized training plan for you and your dog that will help you to understand the reasons for your dog's behaviors, guide you as you train your dog to modify unwanted behaviors, and encourage you to connect with your dog on a deeper level.

APPENDIX E
14-Day Training Journal

	No ("Zee")	Watch	Sit	Climb	Down	Stay	Heel	Stand
Day 1								
Day 2								
Day 3								
Day 4								
Day 5								
Day 6								
Day 7								
Day 8								
Day 9								
Day 10								
Day 11								
Day 12								
Day 13								
Day 14								

Notes:

_____
_____
_____
_____
_____
_____
_____
_____
_____
_____
_____
_____
_____
_____
_____
_____
_____
_____
_____
_____
_____
_____
_____
_____
_____
_____
_____
_____
_____
_____
_____
_____
_____
_____
_____

WOLF KEEPER

TORIANO SANZONE BIOGRAPHY

- Successfully operated two dog training facilities for over six years
- Nominated "2009 Dog Trainer of the Year" by *Tails Magazine* Readers Choice Awards
- Awarded the prestigious PPDA Trainer of the Year Award for 2007 and 2008
- Certified by The American Red Cross in Animal First Aid and CPR
- Creator of the Proof and Certification (P.A.C.) program for canine testing
- First Degree Reiki Healer certified by Master Prama Bhandari
- Invented the Sanzone Style of 12 Doggie Yoga Maneuvers
- Bachelor of Arts Degree in Interpersonal Communication from Gustavus Adolphus College in St. Peter, MN
- Studied animal behavior in Nairobi, Kenya and Kampala, Uganda
- Perfected his dog training skills and concepts while working with various dog-oriented companies:
  — All For Doggie (Doggie Daycare)
  — Bark Chicago
  — Chicago Animal Care and Control
  — Chicagoland Bully Breed Rescue
  — Chicago Canine Academy (Dog Training Co.)
  — Lakeshore Animal Shelter

MASTER WOLFKEEPER TORIANO A. SANZONE
www.thewolfkeeper.com
www.nobegging.com
toriano@thewolfkeeper.com

SANZONE SCHOOL OF DOG TRAINING
910 W. Van Buren St.
Chicago, IL 60607
312-933-1528

This book is property of DOPA DOGS Inc.

WEBSITES TO VISIT
www.thewolfkeeper.com
www.nobegging.com
www.dopadogshop.com
www.akc.org
www.evangersdogfood.com

Made in the USA
Lexington, KY
17 September 2017